W9-DJH-009

Confronting
IRAQ

U.S. Policy
and the
Use of Force
Since the
Gulf War

DANIEL L. BYMAN
MATTHEW C. WAXMAN

Prepared for the
Office of the Secretary of Defense

National Defense Research Institute
RAND

E
183.8
.I57
B9
2000

PREFACE

Although Saddam Husayn's Iraq has regularly defied U.S. pressure, a close look at recent history reveals that Baghdad has also often retreated in the face of U.S. threats or limited military strikes. This mixed record illustrates many of the challenges that commonly arise when confronting major regional adversaries. This report seeks to derive lessons for future confrontations with Baghdad and for coercive diplomacy in general. It examines the nature of Iraq as an adversary, U.S. objectives in the Persian Gulf region, and the historical record of recent attempts to coerce Iraq. It then assesses Iraq's vulnerabilities and concludes by drawing broader implications for successful coercion.

This assessment is intended to inform both policymakers and individuals concerned with the use of force in general and with Persian Gulf security in particular. Policymakers can draw on this assessment in judging how to better coerce Iraq and how to coerce other adversaries elsewhere in the world.

This research was conducted for the Office of the Assistant Secretary of Defense for Strategy and Threat Reduction within the International Security and Defense Policy Center of RAND's National Defense Research Institute, a federally funded research and development center sponsored by the Office of the Secretary of Defense, the Joint Staff, the unified commands, and the defense agencies.

CONTENTS

FIGURES

forcible
constraint
or restraint

Successful coercion, a cornerstone of an effective foreign policy, depends on the proper application of military force. Despite its overwhelming military power, however, the United States often fails to coerce successfully. To help understand this problem, this study assesses attempts to coerce Iraq since the end of the Gulf War in 1991. Although Iraq remains hostile to the United States and its allies, Baghdad has also repeatedly compromised, and at times even caved, in response to U.S. and allied pressure. The story behind this mixed record illustrates Baghdad's strengths and weaknesses and highlights general lessons about limits on the U.S. ability to bring its full power to bear when coercing foes.

AN ANALYTIC FRAMEWORK

Coercion is the use of threatened force, including the limited use of actual force to back up the threat, to induce an adversary to behave differently than it otherwise would. Coercion is typically broken down into two categories: deterrence (stopping an undesired action from occurring) and compellence (reversing an undesired action). In practice, however, distinguishing between these two is difficult. This report draws on both these categories to inform its overall conclusions about coercion.

Coercion is a dynamic process. Just as the United States or another coercer tries to shape Iraq's or another adversary's behavior, so too does Iraq try to reduce the pressure imposed on it. Adversaries typically try to counter-coerce the United States, inflicting military, political, or diplomatic costs to force the United States to drop its threats.

Any assessment of the U.S.-Iraq confrontation must focus equally on the U.S. capacity to apply pressure and on Iraq's capacity to neutralize or reverse it.

Coercive success is often difficult to measure. The same action can have both positive and negative effects, particularly when long-term ramifications are taken into account. Many past studies of coercion have paid inadequate attention to the range of goals pursued by the coercing power. With the same action, the United States can succeed in forcing Iraqi troops off the Kuwaiti border even as it fails to stop Iraq's nuclear, biological, and chemical (NBC) programs. Any study of U.S. attempts to coerce Iraq must recognize the many, often competing, U.S. goals in the region—both short-term and long-term.

Taken together, these points suggest that successful coercion has as much to do with constraints on the coercer as with vulnerabilities of the adversary and that the balance of constraints and vulnerabilities can change over time. Coercing Iraq is not just about threatening it with air strikes and sanctions but about the interaction of two political systems within a broader international context.

IRAQ AS AN ADVERSARY

To understand why coercion succeeds or fails in a given case, it is necessary to understand what drives an adversary's decisionmaking. Iraq is thoroughly dominated by Saddam Husayn and his henchmen: their vulnerabilities and aspirations are, for the purpose of coercion, Iraq's vulnerabilities and aspirations.

Saddam ruthlessly maintains his hold on power, and keeping power is the dominant concern that drives his regime's decisionmaking. All positions of importance are in the hands of carefully selected individuals, who are usually from trusted Sunni Arab tribes or families. Using his numerous and overlapping security services and select military units, the Iraqi dictator has eliminated any potential rivals. These services and units suppress popular unrest and guard against a coup or assassination attempt.

In addition to fear and repression, Saddam uses political measures to solidify his rule. He tries to curry favor with core Arab nationalist supporters by pursuing Iraqi hegemony in the region and Sunni Arab domination within Iraq, objectives that Saddam believes in but also supports for instrumental reasons. Saddam also uses financial rewards to co-opt leading tribal figures and employs the media to trumpet his identity as a powerful leader to impress supporters.

Iraq's strategic objectives reflect both Saddam's personal ambitions and the desires of his core supporters. Four related goals drive Iraq's strategy today: maintaining the current regime's hold on power, ending UN sanctions, achieving regional hegemony, and building an NBC weapons capability. These goals reflect Saddam's desire to end pressures that highlight Iraq's current weakness and his ambition to lead the Arab world.

THE HISTORICAL RECORD

The United States has pursued several, often-competing objectives with regard to Iraq. First, the United States has tried to prevent any Iraqi aggression by keeping Iraq weak and maintaining a strong regional presence. Second, it has sought to reverse Iraq's NBC programs. Third, it has pressed to change the Iraqi regime. A fourth, negative objective has also shaped U.S. policy: preventing instability among its allies that might result from U.S. actions. These four objectives underlie U.S. attempts to coerce Iraq since the Gulf War.

The United States, however, does not have a free hand in its Iraq policy. Washington has long feared that the sudden collapse of Saddam's regime would lead to chaos in Iraq and provide an opening for Iran to increase its influence. Washington seeks to keep its regional and international allies behind its policies, and they often differ on the correct way to confront Saddam. The United States also is ambivalent about its commitment to Iraq's Kurds and Shi'a. Although Washington feels a humanitarian interest in their well-being, it does not want its regional policies tied to these communities. Similar ambivalence can be found in U.S. attitudes toward sanctions. Sanctions are viewed as an effective tool for squeezing Baghdad, but the United States has tried to reduce their impact on the Iraqi populace. Finally, domestic politics shape U.S. actions: no administration can afford charges that it is "soft" on Iraq. Political pressures provide U.S. decisionmakers with military flexibility, but they also limit policy options during crises and when planning for future dangers.

With these objectives and constraints in mind, a close look at the following eight attempts to coerce Iraq or to deter hostile Iraqi actions, sometimes in response to coercion, reveals a mixed U.S. track record:

- Saddam's acceptance of the initial UN Special Commission on Iraq (UNSCOM) inspections at the end of Desert Storm in 1991.

- The imposition of a protectorate over Kurdish-populated areas of northern Iraq in 1991.

- The creation of a no-fly zone over southern Iraq in 1992.

- Saddam's 1992–1993 defiance of both the no-fly zone and UNSCOM.

- The U.S. response to the 1994 Iraqi buildup near Kuwait.

- Saddam's 1996 incursion into the protected zone in northern Iraq.

- The 1997–1998 standoffs over UNSCOM inspections.

- U.S. strikes in response to Iraq's defiance of UNSCOM in December 1998.

Among the positive results, Saddam accepted intrusive UNSCOM inspections for many years after the Gulf War, a safe haven in northern Iraq, and no-fly zones in northern and southern Iraq. More broadly, Iraq has generally refrained from aggression against its neighbors. But despite these concessions, Saddam at times defied the no-fly zones, invaded the northern safe haven, and systematically deceived inspectors.

Coercive threats have contributed to the successful containment of Iraq. Iraq's regional influence, while increased from 1991, remains limited. A robust U.S. regional presence, a rapid surge capacity, and a willingness to use limited force probably have convinced Saddam that regional aggression will not produce results. Coercive threats contributed to containment by maintaining no-fly and no-drive zones and demonstrating regional unity in the face of Iraq's attempts to intimidate its neighbors.

Stopping Iraq's NBC programs has proven far more difficult, but coercive threats have achieved some success. Iraq probably has not attained a nuclear weapons capability, and progress on its biological and chemical programs has probably halted—making this effort at least a partial success when we recognize that, without UNSCOM inspections, sanctions, and other measures, Iraq would probably have a nuclear weapon and a range of biological weapons. Nevertheless, the broader U.S. goals of discovering the extent of Iraq's programs, destroying them, and preventing Iraq from reconstituting them in the future have not been met. Inspectors never discovered the true scope of Iraq's programs, much less destroyed them. Effective inspections ended early in 1998, and even the pretense of arms control has now been abandoned. Although information is scarce, Saddam is probably trying to continue some programs already and certainly will do so once sanctions and isolation end. While threats of force have persuaded Saddam at various times to accept inspections and instances of force have knocked out some of his NBC program resources, the various U.S. actions have not substantially induced a change in Saddam's long-term policies towards acquiring such an arsenal.

Maximal U.S. goals regarding regime change were not met, but Washington's efforts did not destabilize U.S. regional allies as some policymakers feared. Efforts to change the regime—by encouraging Iraqi elites to support a coup or the Iraqi populace to overthrow Saddam—probably are farther from success than at any time this decade. Saddam's position at home appears stronger than in the past, and the Iraqi opposition is fragmented. Coercive threats nevertheless made this goal more realistic. The protected zone in the north, and the humiliations of air strikes, contributed to disgruntlement among Saddam's followers, though not enough to induce a regime change. The United States avoided instability among its regional allies while making the limited progress described above. Saudi Arabia and Turkey, while hardly tranquil, remain loyal U.S. allies. They have supported several U.S. operations in the region without suffering domestic unrest.

U.S. domestic support has been strong with regard to the use of force against Iraq. In general, both the Bush and Clinton administrations enjoyed considerable support from Congress and the U.S. public for their efforts to punish Iraqi aggression and end Iraq's NBC programs. In addition to supporting a large U.S. military presence in the region, the American people have strongly backed policymakers' calls to combat proliferation among rogue regimes. If anything, the American people and U.S. Congress are often more hawkish than the administration leadership. As a result, the President at times has been criticized for not threatening or using enough force.

Allied and international support proved far less consistent than U.S. domestic support and posed a major challenge for U.S. policy. Although U.S. allies in Europe and other major powers initially strongly supported attempts to coerce Iraq, over time France, Russia, and China became increasingly critical of U.S. policy in the region and sought to end or curtail sanctions and inspections. Regional allies often did not support U.S. strikes on Iraq or sought to limit their extent to avoid criticism at home. Lack of consistent regional or allied support undermined the credibility of U.S. threats, encouraged Saddam to defy U.S. ultimatums, and restricted U.S. military options.

IRAQ'S VULNERABILITIES AND COUNTERMOVES

The various U.S. attempts to coerce Iraq reveal that Saddam is most vulnerable, and therefore most likely to give in, when his power base is effectively threatened. Maintaining the support and loyalty of key tribes, Baath party officials, military officers, and other elites is Saddam's overriding concern. When Saddam's power base can be effectively targeted, he is more likely to limit his foreign policy provocations, unless restraint would jeopardize his position at home. After Operation Desert Storm, Saddam's domestic position was weak, and he feared that another blow from the anti-Iraq coalition would shatter it. His response to subsequent threats and weak air and missile strikes in the following years exposed his fear that coalition military strikes might discredit his regime. U.S. military strikes and other forms of pressure that risked humiliating Saddam, demonstrating his inability to respond to U.S. pressure and threatening his control over his power base, proved effective at forcing concessions from the Iraqi regime.

Fear of elite dissatisfaction also helps explain instances when Saddam has issued provocations or refused to back down in the face of U.S. pressure: Saddam was most intransigent when acceding to U.S. demands would decrease support among his power base. In 1996, for example, Saddam saw an opportunity to regain stature in the eyes of core supporters by ordering incursions into northern Iraq against

Kurdish and other resistance forces. Perhaps the most important issue related to elite dissatisfaction is Saddam's commitment to Iraq's NBC programs. Although Saddam's initial defiance on this score may be explained by his belief that deception would triumph over UNSCOM and that sanctions would soon be lifted in any event, eventually the possession of NBC became a source of Saddam's prestige in the eyes of his core supporters.

Saddam is somewhat sensitive to the threat of popular unrest. This sensitivity is largely indirect, though, and arises mostly when unrest risks discrediting him with his power base. Saddam is committed to firm control over Iraq, with his Sunni Arab nationalist brand of chauvinism dominant. The predecessors to the Baath government fell, in part, because they failed to achieve peace at home. Moreover, as Saddam has portrayed himself as the defender of Iraq's integrity (and Sunni Arab hegemony), continued Shi'a, Kurdish, and tribal unrest undercut this source of strength.

The prospect of defeat on the battlefield shapes Saddam's tactics and the nature of his provocations—sensitivity reflected in what Saddam does *not* do rather than in observable Iraqi behavior. Saddam has not threatened his neighbors with military forces since the October 1994 buildup, which the United States countered with Operation Vigilant Warrior. The rapidity of the U.S. buildup, the strong ongoing U.S. regional presence, and the continuing weakness of Iraq's conventional forces probably led Saddam to conclude that another buildup would at best result in an Iraqi withdrawal and at worst in the attrition of his forces. The prospect of military defeat also heightens the chances of both elite dissatisfaction and popular unrest, making Saddam even less likely to issue challenges that could be met on the battlefield. Strikes on military forces could lead officers to become dissatisfied with Saddam, seeing his continued rule as a threat to their lives and prestige.

Saddam does not respond passively to U.S. attempts to target his vulnerabilities and press his regime. Rather, he tries to tailor his response to exploit U.S. weaknesses whenever possible and he takes countermeasures to minimize U.S. pressure. These countermeasures include exploiting domestic suffering, complying incompletely with demands, trying to fracture coalitions, and repressing dissent. These countermeasures (most notably attempts to fracture coalitions) have at times failed or even backfired, but in general the Iraqi leader has managed to offset U.S. coercive pressure.

IMPLICATIONS FOR COERCION

The Iraqi experience is rich with general lessons for coercing major regional powers in critical regions. When designing coercive strategies, policymakers must pay particular attention to the following issues:

- *Recognizing adversary "centers of gravity."* When planning a coercive strategy, policymakers should strive to identify the target's "center of gravity"—that which, if destroyed, would cause the enemy's resistance to collapse. For Iraq, this appears to be Saddam's relationship with his power base. When coercive threats placed pressure on Iraq's center, they proved far more likely to move the regime. A center of gravity, however, will vary by regime and must be assessed and understood accordingly.

- *Recognizing the dynamic nature of coercion.* Coercion is a process, not an event. Planning must acknowledge that just as the United States is (or should be) performing a "center of gravity" analysis on the adversary, the adversary is likely doing the same on the United States or the coalition aligned against it. Because of overwhelming U.S. military capacity, many adversaries may try to undermine public support or fracture U.S.-led coalitions to offset coercive pressure.

- *Understanding what cannot be affected.* The United States can affect only the level of pain it inflicts, not an adversary's willingness to accept it. Adversary regimes are particularly loath to give up power, and coercing populations to revolt or elites to carry out a coup is extremely difficult.

- *Improving long-term planning.* Policymakers and analysts did not anticipate Saddam's survival, and U.S. policy suffered as a result. In future confrontations, the United States should conduct more low-probability, high-impact analysis and "red team" measures to explore the range of possible outcomes and make U.S. policy more robust.

- *Recognizing self-imposed limits.* The attempts to coerce Iraq reveal the degree to which self-imposed constraints, especially those generated by political and diplomatic concerns, limit the quantity and type of force the United States can threaten or use. These self-imposed limits often are far more effective in undermining coercion than are any measures taken by an adversary.

Adopting this framework when confronting adversaries in the future will make coercive threats more sustainable, more robust, and ultimately more effective. Equally important, it will help decisionmakers recognize limits on the use of force and avoid situations where coercive threats will fail in the short-term and undermine U.S. credibility in the long-term.

ACKNOWLEDGMENTS

The authors would like to thank many people for their assistance on this project. F. Gregory Gause III and Thomas McNaugher reviewed this document, strengthening our conclusions and tightening our analysis. Jeff Isaacson and Nora Bensahel also provided valuable input. Richard Kedzior, Gail Kouril, and Jennifer Casey helped locate data for the historical sections of this report. Donna Boykin provided administrative assistance.

Kenneth Pollack, Daryl Press, Gen. John M. Shalikashvili, USA (Ret.), and Judith Yaphe helped provide information on several of the historical cases and offered insights from their knowledge of the region and of U.S. policy. The authors also interviewed several former and current U.S. government officials who asked not to be identified.

Andrew Hoehn and Barry Pavel of the Office of the Assistant Secretary of Defense for Strategy and Threat Reduction provided valuable input and helped focus this report on the issues of greatest concern to policymakers.

ABBREVIATIONS

IAEA	International Atomic Energy Agency
KDP	Kurdish Democratic Party
NBC	Nuclear, biological, and chemical
NFZ	No-fly zone
PUK	Patriotic Union of Kurdistan
SAM	Surface-to-air missile
UAE	United Arab Emirates
UNSCOM	United Nations Special Commission on Iraq
WMD	Weapons of mass destruction

Chapter One

INTRODUCTION

The U.S.-Iraq confrontation since Desert Storm is widely viewed as a frustrating failure for U.S. policy. Iraq remains hostile, committed to its nuclear, biological, and chemical (NBC) programs, and under the leadership of Saddam Husayn, perhaps the world leader America detests most. A closer look, however, reveals many U.S. policy successes. Although Baghdad has repeatedly resisted attempts to moderate its behavior, it has often compromised, or even caved, in the face of U.S. and allied pressure. An examination of these failures and successes offers insight into how to coerce Iraq in the future and how better to conduct coercion in general.

Attempts to coerce Iraq illustrate challenges common to a particular class of foe: major regional adversaries in critical regions. In critical regions, such as the Persian Gulf, the United States is willing to use considerable force to protect its interests. Securing Gulf energy resources has long been a focus of U.S. policymakers. In 1987–1988, the United States and other concerned nations deployed naval forces to the Gulf to stop Iranian attacks on Gulf shipping. When Iranian attacks continued, the United States retaliated, sinking several Iranian naval vessels and destroying offshore oil platforms. In 1991, the United States engaged in Operation Desert Storm, a massive theater conflict involving several hundred thousand U.S. troops, to force Iraq from Kuwait. Since Desert Storm, Washington has maintained a force of thousands of military personnel in the Gulf region and conducted regular, if limited, attacks on Iraq.

Both Democrats and Republicans and the vast majority of the American people recognize that the stakes in the Persian Gulf region are high and that the United States should protect its interests if Iraq or other aggressors threaten the region's security. In the nine years since the Iraqi invasion of Kuwait, the U.S. public has consistently supported various military operations against Iraq. Although opposition to sanctions has grown in humanitarian circles, the U.S. public generally favors a hard line with regard to the use of force against Iraq.[1]

Both in theory and in practice, the recognized vital nature of the U.S. stakes makes successful coercion more likely. First, high stakes give decisionmakers a wide range of military options. While a major theater war to prevent proliferation in the Indian subcontinent or another nonvital region would have little support at home, the United States did, and could again, wage such a war if its interests in the Gulf were directly threatened, confident that the U.S. people would support it. Second, high stakes bolster the credibility of U.S. threats and its willingness to bear costs, including casualties, to back its threats. Washington's regional interests are widely known and understood. The deaths of 19 Americans in the 1996 Khobar Towers bombing did not shake U.S. resolve to maintain a large force in the Gulf even though similar tragedies in Somalia, Lebanon, and elsewhere had led to U.S. withdrawals in the past. Iraq, Iran, or another foe may still challenge the United States, but they will not assume U.S. passivity in response.

This report examines the challenges of coercing Iraq, using this experience to illustrate overall lessons and dilemmas for coercing major regional adversaries in general. Because this class of foe shapes U.S. strategic decisionmaking and defense resource allocations, dealing effectively with such adversaries is critical to U.S. foreign policy. Although every adversary has different pressure points and must be understood individually—a contention strengthened by

---

[1]A *Newsweek* poll taken in the midst of the October–November 1997 United Nations Special Commission on Iraq (UNSCOM) inspection standoff found that 53 percent of Americans favored using force if Iraq refused inspections because of American participation; 82 percent said they would support the use of force if Iraq carried through on its threat and shot down an American U-2 spy plane. By contrast, a poll two years earlier, when American troops first arrived in Bosnia, found that only 40 percent of those surveyed supported the mission, while 55 percent opposed it (Schmitt, 1997). About three-quarters of the public favored the air strikes and cruise missile attacks against Iraq in December 1998 (Operation Desert Fox) (Connelly, 1998).

this report's findings—the lessons from the Iraqi experience also have implications for coercing Iran, North Korea, Libya, and other medium-sized rogue powers in critical regions.

This report's conclusions are primarily directed at the U.S. policy community, particularly in the Office of the Secretary of Defense, trying to design coercion strategies and promote associated capabilities. The findings will also interest policymakers focused on Iraq, as well as a broader audience concerned with using force more effectively in the future.

Chapter One having laid out the purposes of this report, Chapter Two presents an analytic framework for understanding the confrontations with Iraq. Chapter Three describes Iraq as an adversary, depicting how Saddam stays in power and outlining his foreign policy goals. Chapter Four details U.S. objectives in the region and the overall U.S. strategy for achieving them. Chapter Five analyzes eight attempts to coerce Iraq since the end of Operation Desert Storm, paying particular attention to the objectives of the parties involved, the degree of diplomatic support, and the factors that shaped the contest's outcome. Chapter Six draws on these cases to evaluate Iraq's vulnerabilities and how Baghdad tries to minimize coercive pressure. Chapter Seven concludes by examining the broader implications of these findings for coercing major regional powers, noting factors that facilitate success and highlighting likely obstacles.

Chapter Two

UNDERSTANDING COERCION

The confrontations with Iraq since Desert Storm fall into the analytic category of coercion: the use of threatened force to induce an adversary to behave differently than it otherwise would.[1] Coercion is often thought of in terms of an adversary's comparison of costs and benefits for a particular course of action. The assumption is that an adversary will behave in a given way only if it expects a net gain from doing so. By threatening an adversary with costs unless it changes course, a coercer can manipulate its behavior.

With this as a starting point, scholars and analysts typically break coercion down into "deterrence" and "compellence." Deterrence is portrayed as preventing an action from occurring (e.g., convincing Iraq not to invade Kuwait) while compellence is reversing a previous action (e.g., convincing Iraq to withdraw from Kuwait).[2] Such a framework is a useful starting point, but it neglects three important qualifications: that the compellence versus deterrence distinction often breaks down in practice, that coercion is a dynamic process, and that success and failure are often difficult to distinguish.

This chapter first defines coercion and then briefly elaborates these qualifications, as they have important implications for how to think

---

[1]For a more extensive discussion of this topic and how to think about coercion in general, see Byman, Waxman, and Larson (1999). Parts of this chapter are drawn from that work.

[2]See, for example, Pape (1996, pp. 15–16). The two most important works on the subject are Schelling (1966) and George and Simons (1994). Other important works include Hopf (1994), Huth (1997), Morgan (1985), and Shimshoni (1988).

about the U.S.-Iraq standoff and the practice of coercion in general. This chapter provides a conceptual framework for the empirical analysis that follows.

DEFINING COERCION

Coercion is the use of threatened force, including the limited use of actual force to back up the threat, to induce an adversary to behave differently than it otherwise would.[3]   Coercion is not destruction. Although partially destroying an adversary's means of resistance may often be necessary to increase the effect and credibility of coercive threats, coercion relies on the future imposition of costs to move an adversary.   In short, successful coercion is not war-fighting; the target in question still must have the capacity for organized violence, but choose not to exercise it.[4]

DIFFICULTIES IN DISTINGUISHING COMPELLENCE FROM DETERRENCE

Coercion is typically broken down into two subcategories: compellence and deterrence. Compellence involves attempts to reverse an action that has already occurred or to otherwise overturn the status quo, such as evicting an aggressor from territory it has just conquered or convincing a proliferating state to abandon its nuclear weapons programs. Deterrence, on the other hand, involves preventing an action, which has not yet materialized, from occurring in

---

[3]We use this particular definition to emphasize that, as elaborated in this chapter, coercion relies on the threat of future military force to influence adversary decision-making but that limited uses of actual force may form key components of coercion. Limited uses of force sway adversaries not only because of their direct destructive impact but because of their effects on an adversary's perceptions of future force and the adversary's vulnerability to it. There are, to be sure, many types of coercive pressure (sanctions, diplomatic isolation, and so on); unless specified otherwise, we use the term "coercion" to mean *military* coercion.

[4]Coercion can be understood in opposition to what Thomas Schelling termed "brute force": "[B]rute force succeeds when it is used, whereas the power to hurt is most successful when held in reserve. It is the threat of damage, or of more damage to come, that can make someone yield or comply. It is latent violence that can influence someone's choice." Coercion may be thought of, then, as getting the adversary to act a certain way by any means short of brute force (Schelling, 1966, p. 3). See also Pape (1996, p. 13).

the first place. Deterrence would include dissuading an aggressor from trying to conquer a neighboring state or convincing a country that desires nuclear weapons not to seek them.

In practice, however, compellence is difficult to distinguish from deterrence and to separate from the overall security environment. Such haziness often leads to misunderstandings of the inherent role that compellence plays in deterrence and vice versa.

While analysts and academics typically draw sharp distinctions between the two, in practice deterrence and compellence tend to blur, and both ultimately boil down to inducing the adversary to choose a different policy than it otherwise would.[5] Classifying cases as compellence as opposed to deterrence is always speculative to some degree, given the inherent opacity of enemy intentions. And, ultimately, general deterrence and compellence are codependent, as success or failure in coercion affects the coercing power's general reputation to some degree and thus its overall ability to deter.[6]

Figure 2.1 illustrates the difficulty of drawing clear lines between compellence and deterrence. General statements such as "don't invade Kuwait" appear to fall clearly in the deterrence camp, while calls to withdraw would be obvious compellence cases. Yet the in-between areas are more ambiguous. "Don't go further," involves both stopping an existing action and avoiding a future one. Moreover, a call to withdraw carries with it an implicit demand not to engage in the offense again and affects the credibility of the deterrence call not to invade Kuwait in the future. This is not to say that these analytic categories are not valuable, but rather to note that the categories overlap considerably in practice.

---

[5]Some of these observations are elaborated in Schelling (1966, pp. 70–86). Although we argue that the compellence versus deterrence distinction blurs in practice, from a psychological perspective it is often harder for a leader or regime to give up something once they have made the effort to gain it in the first place. See Kahneman and Tversky (1979, pp. 263–291) for more on common decisionmaking biases.

[6]For works on the reputation effects of deterrence and coercion, see Hopf (1994), Huth (1997), Morgan (1985), Shimshoni (1988), Bar-Joseph (1998), and Lieberman (1995). Evidence for the reputation hypotheses is mixed (see Huth, pp. 92–93). In general, the reputation effect is stronger when it involves the same countries or when the region in question is the same.

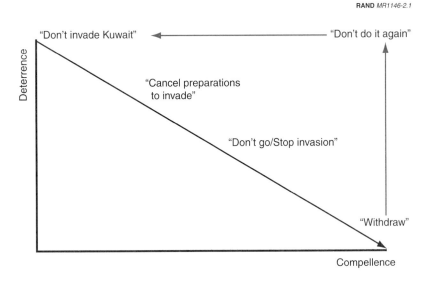

Figure 2.1—Deterrence and Compellence Blur in Practice

The primary focus of this report is on the compellence subset of coercion, but given that deterrence is a highly related phenomenon (both use the threat of force to manipulate an adversary's decision-making calculus), we incorporate insights and examples drawn from both subsets. We use the catchall phrase of "coercion" in the rest of this study.

COERCION AS A DYNAMIC PROCESS

There is a strong temptation to treat coercive threats as single, discrete events, failing to capture the dynamic nature of coercion. This static approach has led analysts to misunderstand causality, which is ultimately where military planners and policymakers most need insight from academics. Analysts instead should view coercive contests as series of moves and countermoves, where each side acts not only based on and in anticipation of the other side's moves, but also based on other changes in the security environment. As noted at the outset, most standard explorations of coercion rely on an expected utility model to determine whether coercion succeeds or fails.[7] These models predict outcomes by comparing the expected costs and benefits of a particular action: coercion should work when the anticipated suffering an adversary associates with the threat exceeds the anticipated gains of defiance.

This "equation" is useful for understanding the problem of coercion in the abstract, but it often confuses the study of coercion when taken as a true depiction of state behavior. One problem is that this equation fosters static, one-sided thinking about coercive contests. It encourages analysts to think about costs and benefits as independent variables that can be manipulated by the coercer, while the adversary stands idle and recalculates its perceived interests as various threats are made and implemented.[8]

A more complete picture requires viewing coercion as a dynamic, two-player (or more) contest. The adversary, too, can move to alter the perceived costs and benefits associated with certain actions. It can divert resources from civilian to military functions, for example, to offset a coercer's attempts to undermine the adversary's defensive capacities. It can engage in internal repression to neutralize a coercer's efforts to foment instability. Rather than simply minimizing the effect of coercive threats, an adversary may try to impose costs on the coercing power. It can escalate militarily or attempt to drive a diplomatic wedge between states aligned against it, perhaps convincing the coercer to back down and withdraw its own threat to impose costs.[9]

Any assessment of U.S. coercion of Iraq should, of course, consider how U.S. threats injected perceived costs into Iraq's decision calculus. But, viewing coercion dynamically, that assessment should also

---

[7]In addition to Schelling's work, a rationalist, cost-benefit approach is employed in many other major works on coercion, including Bueno de Mesquita (1981) and Achen and Snidal (1989). In his study of the effects of strategic bombing as an instrument of coercion, Robert Pape (1996, pp. 15–16) uses such a model.

[8]Pape examines this briefly in his discussion of why Germany did not surrender in World War II. See Pape (1996, p. 256, especially Footnote 4). This point is also implicit in Pape's discussion of how adversaries offset coercive pressure. For a summary, see Pape (1996, p. 24).

[9]For an assessment of such strategies, see Byman and Waxman (1999).

consider Iraq's ability to neutralize those costs as well as to impose costs on the U.S. and its allies.

THE UNCERTAIN MEANING OF "SUCCESS"

Studies of coercion often pay inadequate attention to the range of goals pursued by a coercer. Moreover, they typically employ absolute, binary metrics of success, where a coercive strategy either worked or it failed. Assessments of coercive strategies must shed these tendencies and instead consider a spectrum of possible outcomes.

Classifying a case as a success or failure depends on the particular definition of the behavior sought in that case, leading to confusion when comparing different analyses of the same event. For example, in Operation Desert Storm the behavior sought from Saddam Husayn might have been Iraq's picking up and peacefully retreating from Kuwait. Or, it might have instead simply been Iraq's not being in Kuwait, one way or another. One might conclude that the air campaign successfully coerced Iraq to withdraw from Kuwait because Iraq was willing to withdraw by the end of the air campaign under conditions relatively favorable to the United States. If one instead assumes that coalition objectives were to induce Iraq to withdraw *without having to forcefully expel it* through the use of ground troops, then one could just as easily characterize the air campaign as a failure of coercion.

The way in which the very issue of "success" is framed exacerbates this confusion. The use of absolute, binary terms does not capture the complex and often subtle effects of coercion. Iraq both conceded and defied the United States during Desert Storm. On the one hand, it offered a partial withdrawal from Kuwait as a result of the air campaign while, on the other hand, it refused to accept all U.S. demands. The straitjacket of binary metrics distorts the lessons we may draw from aggregated empirical data when cases in which U.S. threats helped move an adversary in favorable ways but short of maximal U.S. objectives are coded either as absolute failures or as absolute successes.

At the same time binary metrics may bias studies of coercion one way or the other, they may also understate the detrimental effects of coercive strategies. One of the greatest risks of coercion is its potential for backfire. Threatening an adversary may provoke an increase in unwanted behavior rather than the desired course. The 1967 Arab-Israeli War and the 1969–1970 Israeli-Egyptian War of Attrition are frequently cited examples of inadvertent escalation resulting from coercive threats.[10] In Somalia, U.S. Army helicopter strikes on strongman Mohammed Farah Aideed's subordinates not only failed to intimidate General Aideed but may also have provoked anti-U.S. sentiment, contributing to the demise of the American-led operation. In other words, coercive strategies can leave the coercer worse off than when it started. Yet within the binary framework, the worst outcome recognized is the null result: backfires and hardening of adversary resistance are coded just as if coercive threats had no effect.

Conceptually, the dependent variable should be understood as a marginal change in probability of behavior. Against a fluctuating background level of threat (and blandishments, for that matter), the probability of the adversary altering its behavior is never zero. Viewing success in absolute terms, based on observed behavior, ignores this positive probability and classifies all desired behavior as "successful" coercion, regardless of how likely that behavior was prior to the additional coercive threat. Data limits may require a focus on observable behavior, but analysts should not forget that understanding coercion is ultimately about understanding the adversary's decisionmaking process.

This chapter has presented an analytic framework for understanding U.S. attempts to coerce Iraq since the end of Desert Storm. It argued that standard frameworks for understanding coercion, such as the distinction between deterrence and compellence and the use of simple cost-benefit models, are useful for heuristic purposes but often oversimplify a complex reality. It further argued that empirical studies should focus not only on U.S. coercive strategies but also on adversary counterstrategies to them. Taken together, these points suggest that successful coercion has as much to do with constraints on the coercer as with vulnerabilities of the adversary and that the balance of constraints and vulnerabilities can change over time.

---

[10]See Stein (1991) and Bar-Siman-Tov (1991).

Coercing Iraq is not only about threatening it with air strikes and sanctions, but also about the interaction of two political systems within a broader international context. The following chapters apply this expanded framework to the extended U.S.-Iraqi conflict both to further refine our theoretical understanding of coercion and to draw specific policy lessons to protect U.S. interests in the Persian Gulf.

Chapter Three

IRAQ AS AN ADVERSARY

Analyzing the effects of coercive threats requires first understanding the adversary in question. Such an understanding provides insight into why coercion works, not just whether the desired behavior occurred or not. Although generalizations drawn from history and recent related attempts are useful, in practice coercion cannot be universalized: what works for Iraq may fail for China and vice versa. Because Iraq is a country thoroughly dominated by Saddam Husayn and his henchmen, understanding their vulnerabilities and ambitions is critical to designing a coercion strategy. Different states and leaders often will have different priorities even when their behavior appears the same. Thus, the calculations that affect their decisionmaking will vary from case to case.

Information on Iraqi decisionmaking—perhaps the most important variable for understanding how coercion works in practice—is scarce. Fully understanding this decisionmaking requires access to Saddam himself and those close to him. As proximate sources of information, this study has relied on interviews of knowledgeable scholars and policymakers, on Iraqi press and public statements, and on secondary sources from regional experts. These sources tend to emphasize the rational aspects of Iraqi decisionmaking—we know less about bureaucratic and personal rivalries that may also shape Iraqi policies. To be clear, however, our information on Saddam's Iraq is sketchy at best, and thus the conclusions drawn from this report should be reconsidered as new information emerges.

This chapter examines how Saddam stays in power, his overall foreign policy goals, and his strategy for achieving his goals. When appropriate, it notes uncertainties and limits in our understanding of Iraq.

HOW SADDAM STAYS IN POWER

Saddam maintains a firm grip on power. Since assuming power in 1979, Saddam has dominated Iraq's foreign policymaking.[1] The analysis contained here deliberately refers throughout to coercing "Saddam" because efforts to coerce Iraq are largely equivalent to coercing his autocratic regime.

Saddam is particularly careful to keep his core supporters satisfied. Saddam's core supporters consist of members of selected Sunni Arab tribes, certain Baath party officials, and key military and intelligence units. These individuals could, if not carefully controlled, remove Saddam from power through assassination or a coup. Because of his reliance on force to stay in power, the Iraqi leader is not very sensitive to public opinion.

To stay in power, the Iraqi dictator has systematically eliminated potential rivals, either killing them outright or transferring or demoting them to prevent them from developing an independent power base. Although the vast majority of the Iraqi people probably loathes him and opposes his rule, open dissent in areas under the Baath regime's sway is almost nonexistent. The Iraqi media report only Saddam's victories (both real and imagined), and all organizations, even the most innocuous, are carefully monitored by regime security forces.

Security and Regime Protection Forces

Saddam has good reason to fear for his life and the survival of his regime. After Desert Storm, the Kurds rose in northern Iraq and briefly liberated much of it from Saddam's rule—the latest of the major Kurdish rebellions that have occurred regularly since the

---

[1]Saddam formally assumed power in 1979. Saddam, however, gradually consolidated power after the Baath seizure of power in 1968; his 1979 ascension was merely a belated formality. Throughout the 1970s he was probably the dominant voice in Iraqi decisionmaking.

1960s. In several southern cities, Iraqi Shi'a also rose, only to be brutally put down. Through 1996, Iraqi opposition forces were active in northern Iraq, and many groups remain active, though largely in exile, to this day. Although information is scarce, coup attempts occur from time to time, and tribal revolts have become more frequent because of Saddam's repression.[2] Most ominously for Saddam, fighting within Saddam's immediate family has increased. In August 1995, Husayn and Saddam Kamil Hasan al-Majid, both sons-in-law and close associates of Saddam, defected to Jordan, along with their families. Although both returned in February 1996, only to be assassinated, their defection was a blow to Saddam. Saddam's son Uday was shot and badly wounded in December 1996, probably as a result of intrafamily disputes.

Not surprisingly given the regular challenges to his rule, Saddam is well practiced in keeping power. Before rising to the top of the Baath party's ranks, Saddam was an assassin, a party thug, and chief of Iraqi internal security—positions that gave him firsthand knowledge, now essential to his regime's survival—of how to take and keep power. This background has helped him skillfully mix secrecy and terror to keep his opponents intimidated and off-balance (Matlak, 1999).

The primary instruments of Saddam's rule are the ubiquitous intelligence and security services. Aside from Saddam's personal bodyguards, the innermost group is the Special Security Organization. The Special Republican Guard forms the next circle, and it protects Saddam and guards against a military coup by garrisoning Baghdad. Both the Special Security Organization and the Special Republican Guard are headed by Saddam's son Qusay. Various intelligence agencies make up the next circles, each of which is dedicated to rooting out any opposition to Saddam (Ritter, 1999, pp. 122–125). These security services overlap and regularly report on each other. They also rely heavily on deception, fostering false conspiracies in the hopes of drawing out potential traitors. Not surprisingly for a

---

[2]Between 1991 and 1996, there were at least three coup attempts. Moreover, tensions with the Ubayd tribe developed in 1993, and in 1995 elements of the Dulaym tribal federation revolted. Information on the scope and scale of these revolts is lacking. The number of coup attempts may be significantly higher (Baram, 1998, pp. 27, 48–50).

man who has made many enemies, Saddam keeps a close watch on any access to his person. Members of his bodyguard are drawn almost exclusively from Saddam's home area. Other key regime protection assets, such as the Special Security Organization and the Special Republican Guard, also recruit largely from Saddam's al-Bu Nasir tribe and other nearby tribes that have good relations with the al-Bu Nasir (Baram, 1998, p. 25).

A key task of regime protection units is defending against a military coup. The Republican Guard, in addition to serving as elite regime troops, defends the regime against a popular insurrection as well as dissent from regular army forces. As with any other important force in Iraq, the system has built-in checks: the Fedeyeen Saddam, a paramilitary group controlled by Saddam's son Uday that assists in regime security, and the Special Republican Guard both act as a counterweight to the Republican Guard, reducing its ability to carry out a coup (Baram, 1998, p. 50).

Political Techniques

Along with building these protection forces, Saddam relies on several political strategies to solidify his rule. First, the Iraqi leader tailors his foreign and domestic policies to suit the interest of his core supporters. In general, Saddam's core supporters seek to preserve their hegemony in Iraq, to promote Sunni Arab power within the country, and to gain recognition as the dominant Arab power. Saddam shares these ambitions and also exploits them to retain political power.

Second, Saddam strives to keep potential competitors off balance: the same act may yield a reward or an imprisonment, depending on whether Saddam views the actor as a threat or an ally at that moment. Unpredictability is a tool he uses to stay ahead of potential rivals (Matlak, 1999). As Saddam noted to one of his henchmen, "What is politics? Politics is when you say you are going to do one thing while intending to do another. Then you do neither what you said or what you intended." (Cockburn and Cockburn, 1999, p. 7.)

Third, Saddam also uses co-optation and other forms of favoritism to ensure the support of a limited number of partisans. Key regime supporters, particularly among important tribes and families, receive considerable regime largesse despite economic sanctions. The al-Bu

Nasir tribe, in particular, is cushioned from the impact of sanctions (Baram, 1998, p. 24). Indeed, sanctions have in some ways strengthened Saddam's rule, as many Iraqis are facing impoverishment and thus need regime assistance more than ever.

Fourth, the Iraqi leader plays up the image of himself as the leader of the Arabs to bolster support at home. Saddam seeks to project an image of strength whenever possible. He believes that his position depends on maintaining his *sharaf* (honor), which in turn requires dominating any confrontation (Eisentadt and Pollack, 1998). This image of strength, Saddam believes, gives him control at home and influence abroad.

The Iraqi press trumpets the theme that only Saddam can save Iraq. The threat to Iraq—be it Zionists, Persians, the United States, or other foes—varies from crisis to crisis, but the theme of Saddam as savior remains constant. Saddam specifically plays up his success in quelling internal unrest among the Kurds and Shi'a to consolidate support among core supporters (Matlak, 1999).

Saddam is even skilled at "spinning" his failed foreign policies to promote his image as a strong leader. Saddam, who had fled to Egypt after a failed assassination attempt against Gen. Abd al-Karim Qasim in 1959, learned how a leader can play on resistance to the West to drum up popular support (Baram, 1998, p. 39; Matlak, 1999). As Gamal Abdel Nasser of Egypt did before him, Saddam uses his standoffs with the West, even when they end in disaster, to demonstrate his willingness to stand tall (Matlak, 1999).

Finally, the Iraqi leader tries to keep the broader masses of the Iraqi people satisfied with his regime by offering them economic rewards and championing their aspirations for Iraqi hegemony. During the Iran-Iraq war, Saddam tried to keep Iraq's standard of living high, particularly for the families of regime soldiers, to secure their loyalty (Baram, 1998, p. 3). In 1996, Saddam reluctantly accepted UN Security Council Resolution 986, the "oil-for-food" deal, to prevent hyperinflation and economic collapse from further eroding regime popularity.

Saddam's power base has become narrower since the end of the Gulf War. In the past, Saddam had relied on Sunni tribes, particularly those affiliated with his own tribe, family members, the Baath Party, and the army for support. All these pillars are weaker now. After 1995, his power base was probably less united than at any time since the early 1970s (Cockburn and Cockburn, 1999; Baram, 1998, pp. 8, 65–74). Economic sanctions have limited his ability to buy the goodwill of the Iraqi people. The hundreds of millions of dollars Iraq derives from smuggling and from kickbacks from oil-for-food vendors, however, gives the regime some resources to buy goodwill.[3]

IRAQ'S FOREIGN POLICY GOALS

Four major goals drive Iraq's foreign policy today: keeping the current regime in power, ending UN sanctions, achieving regional hegemony, and building an NBC weapons capability.

The overriding concern of the current regime is preserving, and ideally increasing, its power in Iraq—a concern reflected in Iraq's foreign policy. As noted above, Saddam's domestic agenda stresses suppressing dissent and preserving himself and his regime. Iraq's foreign policy shares this emphasis. Efforts to gain influence in the Arab and Muslim world—and to defy the United States—are used at home to burnish Saddam's credentials. Every foreign policy action must be understood both in terms of Saddam's hold on power and Iraq's foreign policy interests.

Saddam seeks the immediate removal of sanctions, more for political than for economic reasons. More than any other issue, sanctions symbolize Iraq's isolation and the persistent Western, particularly U.S., efforts to punish Baghdad. Their removal would signal to Saddam's power base that the Iraqi leader remains unbowed and has emerged triumphant. In material terms, the removal of sanctions would increase the regime's resources and enable Saddam to rebuild his conventional forces.

In the longer term, Saddam seeks regional hegemony and recognition as the leader of the Arab world. Iraq's propaganda, and Saddam's effort to expand his influence through force against Iran and

---

[3]Sales of smuggled goods are not supervised by the United Nations, and thus the money goes directly into the regime's coffers. Iraq also at times sells oil at below-market prices. Middlemen then resell the oil at market prices, passing some of their profit back to the Iraqi regime.

Kuwait, evince a leader committed to expansion. To this end, Saddam built up enormous conventional forces after the Iran-Iraq war, creating the world's fourth largest army before much of it was destroyed in Desert Storm, by subsequent U.S. and allied operations, and by a lack of maintenance due to sanctions (Khalilzad, 1995, p. 108). For Saddam and the Baath party, pan-Arab successes abroad that suggest Iraqi hegemony are also seen as increasing their influence at home (Bengio, 1998, p. 121).

Possessing NBC weapons complements Saddam's regional ambitions. First, they give Saddam a military instrument of proven strength. He can threaten his neighbors or, if necessary, use these weapons to gain an edge on the battlefield as he did in the latter years of the Iran-Iraq war. Both Saddam and his power base believe chemical weapons played a critical role in Iraq's victory over Iran in the Iran-Iraq war. Second, NBC weapons offer a potential counter to the overwhelming U.S. conventional superiority in the region. Third, they are status symbols. As an NBC state, particularly a nuclear one, Saddam's Iraq can plausibly threaten Israel and must be taken seriously by the West. NBC weapons thus force the international community to pay attention to, and by implication respect, Iraq's position in the world. Fourth, and perhaps most important, preserving Iraq's NBC programs is of vital concern to Saddam's power base. As Amatzia Baram (1998) notes, many in the Iraqi security establishment "are incensed at the destruction of their weapons of mass destruction. It is their duty to guard Iraqi national security against two formidable neighbors: Iran and Turkey." NBC systems are seen as both an equalizer with these powers and as a way to counter Israel.

SADDAM'S SHIFTING STRATEGY

Several patterns emerge from surveying Saddam's policies over the past decade. To achieve his foreign policy objectives, Saddam relies on a mix of threats, lies, and promises.

Saddam has repeatedly bullied neighboring powers. He has denounced the regimes of Saudi Arabia, Kuwait, Turkey, and other states that have hosted U.S. troops. He has also occasionally threatened them by building up forces near their borders. Although Saddam's reasoning is not known, he may be seeking to intimidate his foreign foes into compliance as he would internal enemies.

The Iraqi dictator relies heavily on deception to achieve his ambitions. He agreed to UN inspections in part because he believed he could fool UNSCOM as he had fooled the International Atomic Energy Agency (IAEA) in the years before the invasion of Kuwait, during which Iraq built most of its nuclear program (Ritter, 1999, p. 33). Saddam reportedly noted to senior advisors in 1991, "The Special Commission is a temporary measure. We will fool them and we will bribe them and the matter will be over in a few months." (Cockburn and Cockburn, 1999, p. 96.) Even while inspections went on, Saddam denied a major biological program until the defection of the head of the program to Jordan forced him to reveal its extent.

Saddam tends to compromise in the short term, however, when necessary to achieve his immediate aims. He has accepted the UN-demarcated border with Kuwait, agreed to the oil-for-food deal even though it postponed the complete lifting of sanctions, and otherwise accepted the international community's position when his internal base was under siege. In general, Saddam has sought an immediate payoff for any charm offensives and has not engaged in a systematic campaign of wooing foreign powers.

Since the end of the Gulf War, Saddam has turned increasingly to extraregional powers, such as France, China, and Russia, to promote an end to sanctions and Iraq's diplomatic isolation. In November 1997, for example, Saddam briefly retracted his demands that UNSCOM inspections cease when France and Russia warned him that this might impede the removal of sanctions (Baram, 1998, p. 1). Baghdad has also promised contracts and other economic rewards to the firms of states that will help ease sanctions.

Saddam as an Adversary: A Cagey Foe or Foolish Thug?

Although information is too limited to assess Saddam's decision-making with great certainty, several points are clear. First, Saddam is far better at making decisions that concern domestic events than those that concern foreign affairs. The Iraqi dictator has skillfully played off potential opponents at home, exploiting tribal, ethnic, religious, and political differences to maintain power. Saddam often applies the same strategy to foreign affairs as he does to domestic politics, using a combination of revenge, bluster, and brutality (Matlak, 1999). In foreign affairs, however, the mixture of posturing and threats has alienated potential supporters, leading them to support the United States. The United States and its allies can expect cunning at home and blundering abroad.

Second, Saddam is a reasonable short-term diplomatic tactician, but a poor strategist. The Iraqi dictator is able to seize on and exploit the potential benefits of sanctions, infighting among Kurds, and other opportunities thrust upon him. He is far less skilled, however, at creating opportunities to act. He does not appear to plan for the long term or to recognize the long-term costs of short-term actions.

This chapter explored Iraq's unique characteristics as an adversary. Saddam's focus on preserving power and overall foreign policy ambitions greatly affect Iraq's susceptibility to U.S. threats. The following chapter outlines U.S. objectives and politics with respect to Iraq, to set up a dynamic analysis of their extended confrontation since the Gulf War.

Chapter Four

U.S. OBJECTIVES, OPTIONS, ASSUMPTIONS

The end of the Gulf War left the United States in a strong position in the Gulf region. Iraq's military was shattered, and Saddam's regime was reeling. The United States, in contrast, had tremendous prestige, both in the region and in the world. To improve its military position, Washington signed a series of access agreements, sold large quantities of arms to its Gulf allies, and arranged for the presence of substantial U.S. forces in the region.

In subsequent years, the United States has pursued a number of objectives with regard to Iraq, including preventing any Iraqi regional aggression, stopping Iraq's NBC and missile programs, and removing Saddam from power. A negative objective—preventing the spread of regional instability—has also guided U.S. actions.

The relative priority of these goals has shifted in recent years, however, with considerable implications for the success of coercion. Although U.S. priorities have changed, U.S. policy instruments have remained constant. As a result, coercion has been less successful during recent standoffs over NBC weapons, in part because the instruments available to U.S. policymakers were designed to combat regional aggression.

This chapter provides the context for measuring the success of U.S. attempts to coerce Iraq. It first notes important analytic assumptions that shaped U.S. objectives and decisions. It then describes U.S. objectives, discusses the factors required to sustain these goals as well as constraints on U.S. actions, and assesses current challenges to meeting U.S. objectives in full.

ANALYTIC ASSUMPTIONS

Several assumptions have guided and shaped U.S. policy. These assumptions include the following.

- Saddam's imminent demise. The United States and its allies focused on the near term, assuming that Saddam would eventually fall.[1] Analysts and policymakers alike saw Saddam's post–Desert Storm position as weak and believed that a coup or assassination would topple the Baath regime. Continued isolation and economic pressure would hasten this event.

- A foe without honor. Washington assumed—correctly, as later events proved—that Saddam was not to be trusted and that any agreements with his regime would not be honored. Thus, although both the Bush and Clinton administrations pressed Baghdad to accept various UN resolutions and other ultimatums, they also believed that only economic pressure and the threat of military force would lead to successful compliance.

- Caution at home. U.S. decisionmakers believed little public support existed for massive operations against the Iraqi regime, such as a large ground operation. Decisionmakers also feared that even small numbers of casualties would generate opposition to the U.S. presence in the Gulf region both at home and among allies.

- An aggressive Iran. The United States sought to avoid developments that would increase Iran's influence in the region. Washington therefore avoided significant support to Iraqi rebels, particularly Iraqi Shi'a, after Desert Storm out of fear that this might prompt Iran to intervene and seize part of Iraq (Cockburn and Cockburn, 1999, p. 40).

- Concern about the Shi'a. Washington feared that Shi'a dominance in Iraq would lead to greater Iranian influence, which would also threaten U.S. regional allies and stability in general.

---

[1]During Desert Storm, the United States did not plan systematically for the campaign's end, in part because it feared that leaks would unhinge the anti-Iraq coalition (Cockburn and Cockburn, 1999, p. 33).

- Importance of coalitions. U.S. policymakers believed that pre-serving the international anti-Iraq coalition assembled during Desert Storm was necessary to effectively contain Iraq in the aftermath of the conflict.

- Limited Iraqi NBC programs. One assumption that changed (as noted below) was the assessment of the extent of Iraq's NBC pro-grams. The United States mistakenly believed that Operation Desert Storm had destroyed much of Iraq's capability.[2]   The United States also assumed Iraq's program was limited in scope and that, after Saddam's passing, it would no longer be a regime priority.

As discussed below and further in Chapter Five, these assumptions shaped U.S. objectives, determined their relative priority, and guided (as well as constrained) the application of force.

In general, two of these assumptions have changed dramatically since the end of Desert Storm. Saddam's continued survival has led to a reassessment about his longevity: no longer do policymakers expect a coup or an assassin to solve the Saddam problem in the immediate future. In addition, UN inspectors discovered a far more extensive NBC program than was assumed before Desert Storm. Iraq was far closer to a nuclear capability, and had a far more developed biological weapons program, than was originally thought. To a lesser extent, concerns about the Shi'a and an aggressive Iran have fallen, though they still affect U.S. perceptions of events in the Gulf region.

CONTAINING IRAQI AGGRESSION

Initial U.S. policy emphasized containing any Iraqi aggression, pre-venting the worst while hoping that his fragile regime would soon fall apart. Containment, in essence, sought to keep Baghdad weak to prevent it from threatening its neighbors. Because Saddam's Iraq was not trustworthy, containment required stopping Iraq from reconstituting its military forces—both conventional and uncon-ventional.

---

[2]As the Secretary of Defense Richard Cheney testified in the immediate aftermath of Operation Desert Storm, "Saddam Husayn is out of the nuclear business." (Cockburn and Cockburn, 1999, p. 32.)

Containment had five essential elements: sanctions to keep Iraq weak, intrusive inspections of Saddam's NBC and missile programs, diplomatic isolation, limits to Saddam's deployment of forces, and a large Western military presence in the Gulf. These elements worked together to reassure Western allies and to prevent Saddam from threatening his neighbors.

- Sanctions have played a vital role in keeping Iraq weak. Saddam has had to forgo more than $120 billion in revenue because of sanctions—money that could have helped him rebuild his military, develop his NBC programs, or otherwise increase his ability to threaten his neighbors. Moreover, as long as the UN administers the money Iraq receives from oil sales, sanctions limit Saddam's ability to spread his largesse at home and ensure the loyalty of key military and security units. Although Saddam has found ways to evade sanctions—and at times exploits the impact of sanctions to bolster his regime—they nevertheless weaken Iraq's overall power.

- UN inspections have helped prevent Saddam from rebuilding and extending his NBC and missile programs. Although inspectors have failed to fulfill the ultimate goal of removing Iraq's NBC capabilities, they proved far more effective than reliance on the IAEA or other, less-intrusive regimes designed to control NBC weapons.

- Diplomatic isolation has discredited Saddam at home and prevented him from exerting nonmilitary influence on his neighbors.

- Prohibitions on Saddam's ability to deploy his forces, such as no-fly zones in southern and northern Iraq and no-drive zones, discredited Saddam among his core supporters and have made it far more difficult for him to concentrate his military forces.

- Finally, the large U.S. military force in the region—and the ever-present threat of military strikes from the United States and its allies—has helped keep Saddam "in the box."

These elements of the U.S. post–Gulf War containment policy relied heavily on the support of the world's major powers, key regional allies, and the U.S. public. Sanctions and diplomatic isolation required near-universal cooperation to be effective. Intrusive inspections required the backing of the UN Security Council members. Maintaining no-fly and no-drive zones, and the willingness to use force at times, demanded the support of regional states for basing and a domestic consensus approving of the regular use of force against Iraq. Policymakers saw robust support at home as critical to sustaining the policies over the long term.

Several of these elements are currently under assault. Any pretense of inspections ended in December 1998, and for many months before that they were not intrusive enough to disrupt Saddam's NBC programs significantly. Possible successors to UNSCOM are likely to face severe limits to their effectiveness. Russia has harshly criticized UN inspectors, and among the major powers only Britain has supported the U.S. position consistently. The oil-for-food deal (UN Security Council Resolution 986) has enabled Saddam to spend billions of revenue dollars, effectively offsetting much of the pain wrought by sanctions. Although Iraq is hardly a member in good standing of the community of nations, its diplomatic isolation is steadily declining. Finally, the consensus on the use of force against Iraq is in question, as several Gulf allies have at times denied or limited U.S. basing for strikes against Iraq.

The most visible sign of containment's troubles is the contretemps over sanctions. Under current restrictions, the UN must approve Iraq's purchases. Most approved sales are for food, medicine, or other humanitarian necessities and are paid for through sales of Iraqi oil. Iraq cannot purchase arms or technologies related to its NBC programs. Sanctions, however, are seen in the Arab world, including the people of many Gulf allies of the United States, as cruel and senseless, a tool that starves innocent Iraqi children while doing little to Saddam. Uncritical acceptance by some UN members of Iraqi claims of the humanitarian devastation wrought by sanctions (and a failure to recognize that the end of sanctions would not lead Saddam to spend more on the Iraqi people) has made this instrument unpopular in the West as well. Despite U.S. efforts to combat the most pernicious effects of sanctions through the oil-for-food deal, which Iraq accepted only after years of defiance, sanctions are widely seen as unjust and ineffective.[3]

In part because of the perceived devastating effects of sanctions but also because of a vestige of pan-Arab sentiment and hostility toward the West, many Arab governments are increasingly critical of the U.S.-led containment effort. Among U.S. allies, Egypt has led the effort to end containment. Saudi Arabia, Bahrain, and the United Arab Emirates (UAE) also have questioned sanctions and at times objected to certain U.S. military strikes against Iraq. Although the degree of Arab support for U.S. policies has varied according to the winds of domestic sentiment and the level of hostile Iraqi rhetoric, in general opposition to containment or other harsh policies has grown in recent years. Gulf allies are also wearying of the large U.S. military presence. These allies, and Turkey as well, have lived with Saddam in the past and are more accustomed to resolving foreign policy disputes through accommodation than confrontation.

U.S. efforts to contain Iraq also have taken a toll on U.S. military readiness and morale. The United States supports a large military presence in the region (at times since the Gulf War reaching more than 30,000 personnel) and at home dedicated to keeping Saddam in check. Sustaining the no-fly zones in northern and southern Iraq (Operations Northern Watch and Southern Watch, respectively) has drained resources and made it difficult to maintain Air Force training schedules. Perhaps more important, these continuing operations, and the regular surges required to deploy to the region in response to Iraqi provocations, have strained military rotation and leave schedules. The inhospitable welcome often given to Western forces further strains the military. Morale and retention have suffered as a result.

Some domestic and foreign resistance to containment stems from the policy's inability to bring about tangible results. Containment was initially considered a stopgap measure until Saddam fell from power, as he appeared certain to do. U.S. leaders have finally accepted that, absent dramatic outside intervention, Saddam will likely remain in power for years. Saddam appears firmly in charge despite the widespread popular hostility toward his rule and several

---

[3]See Mueller and Mueller (1999) and Gause (1999) for a critique.

coup attempts. U.S. expectations about the regime's fragility, and the subsequent beliefs that a coup could be engineered with relative ease, have proven false. Washington and the rest of the world thus recognize that Saddam's rule may continue for decades, leaving them with the unpleasant choice of living with Saddam in some form or radically shifting policies to promote his ouster.

PREVENTING NBC BUILDUP

Although the conventional military threat Iraq poses remains an important concern, the United States is increasingly focused on Iraq's NBC programs. Before 1990, the world knew little of Iraq's NBC efforts. Information discovered following the Gulf War, however, indicated that Iraq was close to producing a nuclear weapon and had vast chemical weapons stores. Strikes conducted as part of Operation Desert Storm, at the time believed to have destroyed much of Iraq's NBC arsenal and capabilities, did little to set back Iraq's programs. After the defection of key Iraqi regime officials in 1995, however, it became clear that Saddam also had a vast biological weapons program. As U.S. analytic assumptions about Iraq's program proved unfounded, policy changed accordingly.

Given Saddam's unrelenting hostility toward the United States and its allies in the region (both in the Gulf and Israel), his possession of these weapons, which have the capacity to kill hundreds of thousands if properly delivered, became the focus of U.S. policy toward Iraq. A focus on ending Iraq's NBC programs goes beyond containment, which aims to restrict Iraq's behavior abroad. Although the focus on NBC weapons began during the months preceding Desert Storm, the United States elevated the NBC problem to near the top of its concerns, with President Bill Clinton declaring recently that their proliferation "constitutes an unusual and extraordinary threat to the national security, foreign policy, and economy of the United States."[4] In crises in 1997–1998 and 1999, administration spokespeople have emphasized Iraq's NBC programs as their justification for confrontation.

---

[4]Cited in Steinberg (1998).

Like containment, preventing an NBC buildup rests on several pillars. International support is necessary to ensure that Iraq cannot acquire foreign technology and assistance for its NBC programs. Maintaining the strength of inspections and monitoring requires agreement among the major powers at the United Nations. Regional states also are called on for military assistance to degrade Iraq's NBC arsenal. As with containment, however, these pillars are weakening.

TOPPLING SADDAM'S REGIME

U.S. policy is focused on Saddam himself as well as the broader threat that a powerful Iraq poses to the region. U.S. leaders see Saddam as reckless, vengeful, and bloody—dangerous traits for a leader pursuing NBC weapons whose country is astride much of the world's oil reserves. Were Saddam assassinated or removed from power, much of Washington's hostility toward Iraq would be mitigated even though any successor would be scrutinized to see if he is following Saddam's path. After years of waiting for a coup or assassination, the United States is more actively seeking Saddam's overthrow, no longer believing that his demise is imminent. Caution at home, however, has led Washington to avoid the direct involvement of U.S. ground troops or aid to the Iraqi opposition that would require a major U.S. commitment.

According to its rhetoric at least, the Clinton administration is now committed to working with the Iraqi opposition to topple the regime in Baghdad, even as it continues to contain Iraq. In November 1998, President Clinton embraced the Iraqi opposition, promising to work for "a new government" in Baghdad. National Security Advisor Samuel Berger echoed the president, saying that the administration seeks to "strengthen the Iraqi opposition" because containment might not be sustainable and because Saddam's continuation in power is detrimental to U.S. interests (Gellman, 1998). To this end, the administration designated groups eligible to receive U.S. assistance and appointed a special representative for transition in Iraq, Frank Ricciardone, to coordinate U.S. assistance to the various Iraqi opposition groups.[5]

---

[5]So far, the Clinton administration appears to be moving cautiously with regard to the opposition. The 1998 Iraq Liberation Act authorizes the administration to transfer $97

As with other U.S. objectives, regime change depends heavily on regional assistance. Regional powers are needed to provide bases, training, and support for opposition fighters. Equally important, they must host substantial U.S. military forces that would protect and assist the opposition effort—a presence far larger than the already-considerable U.S. forces in the region. Regional states, however, have expressed little support for an opposition-based regime change strategy.[6]

PRESERVING REGIONAL STABILITY

The United States has sought to preserve regional stability even as it pursued ambitious objectives regarding Iraq. Washington feared that instability in Iraq, particularly with Iraq's Kurdish population, could spread to such U.S. allies as Turkey. The United States also strove to avoid any unrest that might increase Shi'a influence in Iraq, fearing that this would strengthen Iran's hand.

Over time, U.S. policymakers have recognized a tension between the use of force and the stability of U.S. allies. Large increases in force, or the regular use of force against the Iraqi regime, angered many radicals in the region, threatening the stability of U.S. allies and the lives of U.S. personnel. The large and highly visible U.S. presence in the Gulf proved a magnet for critics of Gulf regimes, particularly in Saudi Arabia, and radicals in general. Terrorist attacks against U.S. servicemen that resulted in the deaths of five Americans in 1995 and 19 in 1996 highlighted the lethal nature of this threat. In response, Washington often limited the use of force and the scope and visibility of the U.S. presence.

---

million in military equipment to several opposition groups and to assist Iraqi opposition radio and television broadcasts. In addition to this modest aid, the administration is also trying to help the opposition better organize itself. The administration has not, however, committed U.S. military forces to supporting the opposition's cause.

[6]For a critique of an opposition-based strategy, see Byman, Pollack, and Rose (1999) and Byman (1999a).

CONSTRAINTS ON THE UNITED STATES

The United States does not have a free hand in the Gulf region. In particular, five concerns complicate the application of force or limit policy options: fear of Iraqi fragmentation, discomfort with sanctions, a desire to preserve an international alliance, ambivalence about humanitarian objectives, and domestic pressure opposed to any U.S. concessions with regard to Iraq.

Fear of Iraqi Fragmentation

Preventing the collapse of the Iraqi state has long been a major goal of U.S. policy. If Saddam fell suddenly from power, Iraq's tribal confederations, religious communities, and ethnic groups would gain greater autonomy. There is little love lost among these groups. Iraqi national identity is weak in comparison to religious or tribal identity, and the collapse of the center could lead to complete disintegration. Moreover, Saddam Husayn has devastated Iraqi civil society, destroying any independent organization and rending ties among citizens. If Saddam Husayn falls, as Marine Corps Gen. Anthony Zinni, commander in chief of the U.S. Central Command, has testified, dozens of opposition groups might compete for power, destabilizing Iraq (Associated Press, 1999).

The descent of Iraq into chaos could worsen the humanitarian crisis in Iraq.[7] There is no guarantee that Iraq would collapse into neat Kurdish, Shi'a, and Sunni states—and even if it did, they might fight over territories where communities are mixed or where significant oil reserves lie. In Afghanistan, Liberia, Somalia, and elsewhere, the collapse of the central government has made disease, warfare, and

---

[7]From a U.S. point of view, however, a collapse is less calamitous. A weak Iraq would be unable to threaten its neighbors or mount an ambitious weapons of mass destruction (WMD) program. Indeed, various rump states would probably focus their hostility on each other, not on the other states of the region. Given Tehran's military weakness and ideological exhaustion, the United States could easily prevent Iran from dominating any successor state. Moreover, several possible successor states, particularly one dominated by Iraqi Kurds, might become a staunch U.S. ally in the region. Nor is it clear that the humanitarian problems caused by civil strife would be worse than the suffering inflicted by Saddam Husayn's tyranny, which has caused immense suffering and hundreds of thousands of lives. The destabilization of Iraq may be worth the price to be paid for Saddam Husayn's removal. See Byman (1996) for more on this.

banditry far more prevalent. Iraq's collapse could also spread unrest throughout the region, unleashing sectarian and ethnic struggles in Iran and Turkey. Guns and armed fighters might flow across the already porous borders, strengthening resistance groups in these countries.

As a result, U.S. policymakers have sought to avoid policies that might destabilize Iraq. They hesitated to support popular resistance to Saddam in the immediate aftermath of Desert Storm. In addition, they have consistently preferred a coup as a means of regime change, as this would be more likely to leave a strong government in power than would other methods.

Discomfort with Sanctions

The United States and its allies are ambivalent about the sanctions imposed on Iraq. Sanctions were initially imposed as a pressure tactic following the Iraqi invasion of Kuwait. Their continuation throughout the entire decade was not expected by either Iraqis or U.S. policymakers. Regional states are especially skeptical of both the efficacy and the morality of sanctions. Thus, Washington has tried to shore up sanctions to keep Iraq weak while supporting considerable changes in the sanctions regime for humanitarian reasons.

Although the actual impact of sanctions on Iraq is controversial, Baghdad has portrayed their impact as devastating. Saddam has successfully attributed the collapse in the Iraqi standard of living to sanctions rather than to his regime's policies. By manipulating the access of the media and humanitarian organizations, the Iraqi regime has created a widespread perception throughout the world that thousands of Iraqi children are dying each month as a result of sanctions. This has generated considerable opposition to sanctions among U.S. allies. It has also contributed to regional, and to a lesser extent U.S. public, disaffection with U.S. policy.

The United States walks a fine line with regard to sanctions. On the one hand, it seeks to use sanctions to keep Iraq weak, prevent it from acquiring NBC and military-related items, and ratchet up pressure against the Iraq regime. On the other hand, it tries to minimize the impact of sanctions on the Iraqi people (or at least be seen as such in the region and the world) by supporting humanitarian exceptions.[8]

Preserving an International Alliance

The United States seeks to preserve the alliance against Iraq forged during the Gulf War. Several core elements of the U.S. containment of Iraq, particularly sanctions and UN inspections, have depended on international support. Without the support of other major powers, sanctions would have little or no impact. UN inspections also require the support of the Security Council. Furthermore, Washington believes that international support increases the legitimacy of U.S. policy in general, helping sustain the backing of key regional states such as Saudi Arabia and Turkey.

Maintaining an international alliance, however, places severe limits on U.S. freedom of action. With the exception of Britain, allies have tended to be far more skeptical of the need to use force against Iraq. U.S. allies have also been more critical of the humanitarian impact of sanctions. Since 1997, China, France and particularly Russia have also expressed their opposition to a robust inspections regime. Washington must often soften its policy toward Iraq or risk jeopardizing the anti-Iraq alliance.

Humanitarian Ambivalence

The United States and its allies have taken steps to protect Iraqi Shi'a and Kurds from the depredations of Saddam's regime, but these steps are limited and evince a weak commitment to this objective. Washington has avoided any formal commitment to either the Kurds or to the Shi'a, even as it has supported UN resolutions on their behalf to protect them from Saddam's aggression. In both cases, Washington waited until an outcry in U.S. and international public opinion before acting.

---

[8]Saddam rejected the oil-for-food approach for several years, hoping to exploit the suffering to end all sanctions in Iraq. Growing domestic discontent, however, led Saddam to accept the UN resolution in November 1996 (Baram, 1998, pp. 68–74).

U.S. ambivalence stems from both ideological and practical concerns. Washington feels little sympathy towards the Kurds, who have few constituents among the U.S. people and who war with each other as much as with Baghdad. Washington is also concerned that any commitments will be difficult to back up should Saddam make a concerted effort to repress these groups. The United States is perhaps even more reluctant to protect Iraqi Shi'a. Because of Iran's long-standing ties to Iraqi Shi'a and the growth of radical Shiism in Iraq in the 1970s and 1980s, Washington has long feared that greater Shi'a influence in Iraq would either turn Iraq into a radical power, lead it to tilt toward Iran, or both. Regional allies are especially concerned about the growth of Shi'a influence in Iraq. Saudi Arabia and other Gulf states have long feared Iran's revolutionary government, seeing it as seeking to extend its influence over the region, particularly in such Shi'a-populated areas as Bahrain, Kuwait, and Saudi Arabia's Eastern Province.

Domestic Limits to Any Concessions

Both the Bush and Clinton administrations succeeded in forging a solid domestic consensus behind the need to keep Saddam Husayn contained, creating considerable support for any confrontation. The price of this success, however, is severe limits on the U.S. ability to make concessions to Iraq. Any tactical retreats are subject to criticism in Congress and in the media for being "soft" on Iraq. Any administration often must respond to limited Iraqi provocations to sustain domestic support even when the effectiveness of the response is questionable and the U.S. attacks may alienate vital allies.

The above U.S. objectives and constraints provide the context for measuring the success or failure of U.S. attempts to coerce Iraq, which are explored in the following chapter. U.S. coercive threats were designed to further U.S. objectives regarding containment, NBC programs, regime change, and preventing regional instability. At times, coercion was used to preserve or enhance one of the pillars upon which these overall objectives rested. U.S. efforts since Desert Storm have focused both on improving the U.S. position in the region and on preventing Iraqi attempts to discredit and counter-coerce the United States. The impact of U.S. pressure, however, is often softened both by Saddam's responses and by self-imposed constraints on U.S. actions.

Chapter Five

ATTEMPTS TO COERCE IRAQ:
THE HISTORICAL RECORD

A close look at the various confrontations with Iraq after the Gulf War reveals a mixed U.S. track record. On the positive side of the ledger, Saddam accepted intrusive UNSCOM inspections (at least for many years after the Gulf War), a safe haven in northern Iraq, and no-fly zones in northern and southern Iraq. More broadly, Iraq in general has refrained from aggression against its neighbors. On the negative side, Saddam at times defied the no-fly zones, invaded the northern safe haven, and systematically deceived inspectors. He also remains committed to gaining regional hegemony and developing his NBC capacity, while his hold on power appears secure.

This mixed record reveals that the question, "Can Saddam be coerced?" is misguided; clearly he has been to some degree and probably can be again. The more important questions are under what conditions, and for what issues, is coercion likely to succeed or fail. To answer these questions, this chapter examines eight attempts to coerce Iraq or to deter hostile Iraqi actions in response to coercion:

- Saddam's acceptance of the initial UNSCOM inspections at the end of Desert Storm in 1991.

- The imposition of a protectorate over Kurdish-populated areas of northern Iraq in 1991.

- The creation of a no-fly zone over southern Iraq in 1992.

- Saddam's 1992–1993 defiance of both the no-fly zone and UNSCOM.

- The U.S. response to the 1994 Iraqi buildup near Kuwait.

- Saddam's 1996 incursion into the northern protectorate.

- The 1997–1998 standoffs over UNSCOM inspections.

- U.S. strikes in response to the defiance of UNSCOM in December 1998.

Several of these cases fall more on the deterrence side of the compellence-deterrence spectrum, while others fall squarely on the compellence side. All these cases, however, represent instances where the United States used force in an attempt to alter Iraq's decisionmaking and thus are appropriate for the study of coercion.

For each of these cases, the following issues, among others, are analyzed: the provocations, U.S. objectives, diplomatic support, military options, and immediate and long-term outcomes. Each case also assesses probable Iraq motives, though a lack of data makes these assessments informed speculation, not established fact.

This report focuses on attempts to use military force to coerce changes in Iraqi behavior. Therefore, it does not directly examine the issue of whether sanctions have forced concessions from the Iraqi regime or judge the impact of diplomatic isolation.[1] When weighing the effects of force, however, it is vital to remember that sanctions and isolation were operating in the background as coercive instruments. At times, they heavily conditioned Iraq's behavior, leading it to defy the United States when the pressure became too much or, at times, to acquiesce more readily.

For each case examined, domestic support was strong with regard to the use of force. In general, both the Bush and Clinton administrations enjoyed considerable support in Congress and among the U.S. public for their efforts to punish Iraqi aggression and end Iraq's NBC programs. In addition to supporting a large U.S. military presence in the region, the American people have strongly supported

---

[1]See Byman, Pollack, and Waxman (1998, pp. 134–135) for an assessment of sanctions' contribution to coercion.

U.S. policymakers' calls to combat proliferation among rogue regimes. If anything, the American people and U.S. Congress are often more hawkish than the U.S. leadership. As a result, President Clinton at times was criticized for not threatening or using enough force.

ESTABLISHING UNSCOM INSPECTIONS (1991)

Following the end of Desert Storm, the U.S.-led coalition sought to coerce Iraq to fulfill various UN resolutions, including UN Security Council Resolution 687, which called for Baghdad to eliminate its NBC programs. Under the terms of 687, Iraq was to inventory its chemical and biological weapons programs and stock and all material related to nuclear weapons and ballistic missiles. Iraq's military weakness initially gave it little choice but to acquiesce in permitting the inspections (Cowell, 1991). For more than a year following the end of Desert Storm, however, Iraq resisted UNSCOM inspections and refused to cooperate with inspectors in any way. Inspectors nonetheless made progress in uncovering the extent of Iraq's NBC programs, but Iraq's continued resistance and deception prevented a full accounting of Iraq's NBC programs.

In response to Iraqi harassment of inspectors and refusal to cooperate, the United States and Britain (and at times France) threatened bombing campaigns several times in 1991 and 1992. The United States used its military presence in the region, which it occasionally bolstered, to back up threats. During a standoff in March 1991, the United States sent the carrier *America* and its battle group to the Gulf as an escalation option—a particularly potent threat given the large U.S. ground presence then in Iraq itself and along its borders. In September 1991, President Bush sent combat aircraft and Patriot missile batteries to Saudi Arabia after Iraq temporarily detained 40 UN inspectors. In these cases, Washington apparently was weighing a graduated bombing campaign to force Iraqi compliance.

Iraq backed down as a result of these threats, accepting inspectors and making limited declarations. Nevertheless, Baghdad still continued its deception campaign, hiding its weapons and claiming that any known stocks and systems were destroyed during the war. Iraq's continuing recalcitrance suggests that it is highly committed to retaining an NBC capacity and would resume its programs once inspections ended.

U.S. Objectives. The United States and its allies sought to coerce Iraq to fully disclose its NBC programs and to allow unfettered UN inspections to oversee their destruction. Washington also sought to prevent any future Iraqi NBC programs, both by destroying Iraq's capabilities and by obtaining guarantees that Baghdad would not try again.

Although U.S. objectives regarding NBC weapons remained constant, they grew in relative importance in the months following Desert Storm. The scale of Iraq's NBC program, thought to be rather limited before and during Desert Storm, was revealed as massive after the war. Iraq's chemical arsenal was larger than originally believed, and Baghdad also had a far more extensive nuclear weapons development program that was closer to achieving success than Western analysts assessed before Desert Storm. (Iraq also had a major biological weapons program, but its extent was not revealed until August 1995, when Saddam's son-in-law Husayn Kamil Hasan al-Majid, who oversaw Iraq's nonconventional weapons programs, defected to Jordan and revealed many details.) At the same time that NBC prevention gained attention in U.S. policymakers' minds, it became apparent that Baghdad was not cooperating with inspectors and was trying to conceal details about its various programs. On June 27, 1991, Secretary of State James Baker announced an "extraordinarily serious" Iraqi attempt to hide nuclear materials from inspectors.

Iraqi Objectives. Iraq sought to retain its NBC programs despite international pressure. Saddam probably believed that a mixture of denials and deceptions would either fool or satisfy the international community, as it had the IAEA previously. Based on the tepid criticism he received for chemical weapons use in the past, he may also have thought that token cooperation would satisfy the more cynical major powers. Saddam's motivations may have been a mix of general prestige concerns about backing down and a particular desire to retain NBC weapons because of their status-conferring potential and proven ability to threaten his enemies.

Diplomatic Support. Following Desert Storm, the United States had considerable international support for its goal of ending Iraq's NBC programs. The UN Security Council regularly passed resolutions and made statements demanding that Iraq declare and then abandon its NBC programs, and developing world nations and major powers both supported these resolutions. This support also extended to military strikes. On July 14, 1991, Paris indicated its support for military strikes against Iraq if Baghdad continued to seek nuclear weapons, and four days later, Soviet leader Mikhail Gorbachev declared that Iraq should not gain a nuclear capability. In September 1991, Britain and France joined the United States in considering a plan to send military escorts for the inspectors. Turkey, Saudi Arabia, and other regional states also supported the inspections. These countries hosted a considerable U.S. military presence, which was dedicated in part to backing up the UNSCOM effort (Djerejian, 1991).

Comprehensive sanctions on Iraq and inspections were directly linked. Iraq repeatedly demanded the end of sanctions as the price for full compliance with NBC-related UN resolutions. Western diplomats, however, successfully reversed this bargain, using sanctions to force Iraqi compliance and declaring that sanctions would not end until Iraq met the terms of other UN resolutions, including Resolution 687.

Outcomes. The introduction of UNSCOM inspectors to Iraq was a limited coercion success for the United States. Through the inspectors, Washington discovered reams of information about Iraq's NBC programs. In addition, inspectors oversaw the destruction of large amounts of nuclear, chemical, and missile-related materials.[2] Perhaps most important, the continual presence of inspectors and associated monitoring made it far more difficult for Saddam to continue producing chemical and biological agents and to rebuild his nuclear and missile programs.

UNSCOM inspections, however, were an incomplete success even in their early days. Iraq remained committed to its programs. Through

---

[2]UNSCOM has uncovered and destroyed an array of missile systems and chemical weapons, as well as more limited numbers of biological systems. See http://www.un.org/Depts/unscom/achievement.htm for a more complete listing. (Accessed on April 14, 1999.)

deception and defiance, Saddam has kept his programs alive and probably retains some weaponized agents and limited numbers of missiles and launchers. The scientists and engineers who designed the weapons could easily do so again, given the resources. In any event, given the tenacity with which Saddam has resisted inspections, it is clear that the Iraqi dictator is committed to Iraq's NBC programs and will rebuild them if given a free hand. This attempt at coercion also collapsed as the years progressed. Saddam became more and more resistant to inspections (discussed below), particularly after various deception campaigns began to fail. In short, he was coerced in 1991 to accept U.S. demands, but the degree of compliance even then was limited, and it diminished subsequently.

Assessment. Saddam showed himself extremely sensitive to U.S. threats of force. Although he later proved he could weather a limited U.S. bombing campaign, U.S. credibility was high in the days following Desert Storm—both in terms of resolve and capabilities—and Saddam's prestige at home was at its lowest point ever. Strong allied support also made it easier to threaten Iraq effectively.

The long-term goals of preventing an NBC-armed Iraq did not neatly mesh with available instruments. On January 15, 1992, then CIA Director Robert Gates contended that Iraq could rebuild its NBC weapons and missile programs within a few years. Neither Bush nor Clinton administration officials made clear how even the success of UNSCOM in discovering and destroying Iraq's NBC programs, an ambitious goal policymakers did not expect to meet fully, would prevent their renewal once UNSCOM departed. Given the IAEA's repeated failures to prevent determined proliferators from making progress on NBC weapons—and Iraq's successful deception of UNSCOM over the years—expecting complete success with respect to the latter goals was optimistic.

The limited nature of the U.S. success demonstrates problems inherent to coercing an adversary with regard to NBC-related issues. When deception is relatively easy, as it is with most NBC items, and when an adversary is committed to possessing them, then coercing successfully is extremely difficult. Stopping Iraq's future programs over the long term without changing the government of Iraq, Baghdad's regional security postures, or the country's scientific-industrial base may be impossible. Better intelligence on Iraq's program would have required a more substantial on-the-ground presence, which had little support among U.S. allies or at home.

Judging compliance with NBC-related ultimatums also is difficult. Given that much of the equipment, technology, and personnel for these programs falls in the "dual-use" category, it is difficult to decide when a program has ended. States more sympathetic to Iraq could thus more plausibly argue that Iraq's programs were sufficiently reduced or curtailed.

With hindsight, it is clear that the United States initially was playing a short-term game despite the long-term nature of the stakes involved. When Resolution 687 was passed, reports in the press indicated that Baghdad's compliance, which was generally assumed, would clear the way for an end of the embargo (Cowell, 1991). As one interlocutor noted, "687 was not an arms control arrangement. It was part of the conditions for Iraq's surrender." (Shalikashvili, 1999.) The original timetable for the inspection and destruction of the NBC programs was 120 days, after which the ban on Iraqi exports would be reviewed (Sciolino, 1991). Any long-term concerns would be considered in light of Saddam's successors, as it was widely assumed that his regime would fall. This short-term perspective clouded the extent of Iraq's programs and Saddam's determination to retain them.

CREATING A KURDISH SAFE HAVEN (1991–1992)

Immediately after Desert Storm, Iraq's Kurdish minority rose against the Baath regime. On March 22, 1991, the regime began its counteroffensive. Iraqi Army attacks on rebels and civilians in northern Iraq caused massive casualties and suffering among Iraqi Kurds. Tens of thousands of Kurds died as the central government reestablished itself, and over one million Kurds fled their villages toward Iran or Turkey, many ending up stranded without food or shelter in the mountains of northern Iraq (McDowall, 1996).

To alleviate the crisis, the United States dispatched troops in April 1991 to create a "safe haven" for returning refugees. UN Security Council Resolution 688 authorized the use of force to protect relief efforts in the Kurdish north. U.S., French, and British forces set up a "safety zone" and secured refugee camps in northern Iraq. By the end of May 1991, many Kurds in Turkey had returned to Iraq, and Kurds displaced within Iraq had returned to their homes. In May, the United Nations assumed authority for the relief operation.

The United States directly, but reluctantly, intervened to protect the Kurds. More than 10,000 U.S. Army, Navy, and Air Force personnel participated in Operation Provide Comfort, and allied countries contributed approximately 11,000 more. While U.S. and allied forces were in the country, the Iraqi campaign stopped. In addition to securing the safe haven, the United States also established a force in Turkey to deter Iraq and to protect the Kurds (Kelly, 1991; Djerejian, 1991). Even after the UN assumed control of the relief effort, an implicit U.S. military commitment remained.

The confrontation did not end after the creation of the protected zone. In August and September, Iraq began to threaten the enclave, building up troops in the north and conducting forays against the Kurds. Firefights between Iraqi forces and Kurdish paramilitary groups were common. After U.S. threats to retaliate, however, Saddam backed off and did not challenge the enclave directly until 1996 (discussed below).

In general, Iraq showed tremendous respect for U.S. power. After the successes of Desert Storm, Baghdad probably feared renewed attacks if it pushed too hard. Indeed, Iraq not only abided by the terms of Resolution 688, but it also evacuated military forces from all of the Kurdish north, wrongly assuming that U.S. airpower protected the entire region.

U.S. Objectives. The primary U.S. objective in the creation of the enclaves was humanitarian: Washington sought to succor the Kurds, protecting them from the Baath regime's oppression.[3] A related goal was to reassure Turkey, which feared a massive influx of Iraqi Kurdish refugees. In part, the U.S. political leadership's actions were reactive. After the stunning successes of the Gulf War, the sight of thousands of Iraqis fleeing Saddam's repression provoked outrage in the United States, leading to charges that the United States has "won

---

[3]Secretary of Defense William Perry later noted, "Our interest in the Kurds is not a vital national security interest. It's a humanitarian interest." As cited in "Evolution of U.S. Policy on Iraq" (1996).

the war but lost the peace." Such criticisms led the Bush administration to act.

After establishing the enclave, the Bush (and subsequently the Clinton) administration capitalized on its existence to press Saddam further. By playing up the plight of the Kurds, the international community remained focused on Iraq's abysmal human rights record and thus on the need to keep Iraq under sanctions and isolated diplomatically. In addition, the enclave became a base for the U.S.-backed Iraqi opposition and for U.S. intelligence operatives seeking to foment a coup.

Iraqi Objectives. In putting down the revolts and causing the refugee flows, Saddam was pursuing a standard Baath objective of ensuring Sunni Arab domination. As he had after previous Kurdish revolts in 1974–1975 and during the 1980–1988 Iran-Iraq war, Saddam clamped down brutally on Kurdish unrest. He probably sought to regain control to prove to his supporters that he would guard Iraq's integrity and the Sunni Arabs' elite position.

Diplomatic Support. The extraregional members of the U.S.-led Gulf War coalition strongly supported the creation of the enclave in northern Iraq. European nations, not the United States, led the effort to create the safe haven. French leaders took the initiative for creating the no-fly zone, and British Prime Minister John Major formally put forth the proposal to create a haven for refugees. Other European leaders strongly backed these calls for assisting the Kurds. The suffering of the Kurds received tremendous media attention in Europe, making this issue a political priority (Riding, 1991).

In the region, Turkey supported a relief effort, albeit a short-term one with limited scope. Ankara feared that an influx of Kurdish refugees into Turkish territory, or even a mass of Kurdish refugees on its border, would exacerbate Kurdish unrest in Turkey itself. Turkish leaders, however, were quite wary of the creation of a safe haven for the Kurds, fearing the eventual creation of a Kurdish state in Iraq, which would in turn arouse Kurdish nationalism in Turkey. President Turgut Ozal stated that Turkey's security interests required the maintenance of Iraq's territorial integrity: fragmentation into several ethno-religious-political entities would threaten Turkey's own territorial integrity (Sayari, 1991, p. 142).

Many Arab states did not favor the creation of a safe haven for the Kurds. The Arabs sympathized with the Kurds' suffering, but they opposed any plan that might contribute to dismembering a major Arab power. Not only would the region's balance of power be upset, but such action was reminiscent of the colonial past. Many Arabs also accused the West of a double standard, hypocritically aiding the Kurds while the Israelis were allegedly "destroying" the Palestinians (Watts, 1991).[4]

The United States and its allies chose, however, not to create a de jure protectorate or enclave in northern Iraq. Bowing to the sensitivities of Turkey and Arab allies, the coalition avoided the creation of a political entity that could lead to an independent Kurdistan. Such a step would have provided clearer justification for subsequent military enforcement actions—any Iraqi armed assaults into the enclaves might then be viewed as acts of aggression, and not a matter of internal Iraqi security—but it would not have enjoyed diplomatic support in the region (Scheffer, 1991, p. 164).

At the time, the coalition avoided any similar measures to protect the Shi'a of southern Iraq, despite the equally brutal campaign waged against them. U.S. and regional leaders feared that aid to the Shi'a would inadvertently foster Iranian influence in Iraq. In addition, the concerns of Iran regarding refugees and instability carried little weight in Western capitals, in contrast to the concerns of Turkey.

Outcomes. Operation Provide Comfort succeeded in its humanitarian and diplomatic goals. It not only stopped the flow of refugees, but it prompted most refugees to return to their homes. The persecution of the Kurds ended, and Turkey was reassured as to cross-border stability. The Kurds held elections and, even when infighting led to clashes, they remained ruled by their own leaders rather than by the Baath. Similarly, UN spending and aid increased the region's standard of living far more than it would have risen had the Baath controlled it.

Provide Comfort had the unintended, though soon exploited, effect of embarrassing Saddam and providing a way to strike at his regime.

---

[4]This according to Karim Shakar, Bahrain's ambassador to the United Kingdom, and Dr. Omar al-Hassan, director of the Gulf Centre for Strategic Studies.

The northern protected area soon became a launching point for various opposition forays against Saddam and for Iraqi defectors to gather and plot. Perhaps more important, the enclave's continued existence punctured the illusion that Saddam could prevent threats to Iraq's unity.

Assessment. As with the imposition of UNSCOM inspections, Saddam showed himself exceptionally sensitive to the threat of force. Despite the tremendous importance of regaining control over the Kurdish north, Saddam tried to avoid any clash with U.S. forces and even removed his troops from parts of the north not under the protection of U.S. air cover. U.S. credibility was still at a high point, and the visible U.S. armed presence in northern Iraq demonstrated a robust U.S. commitment.

As with inspections, the creation of the enclave in northern Iraq suffered from uncertainty as to the likely duration of the operation. The initial operation was humanitarian in focus. Only when the immediate crisis was resolved did the question of the enclave's ultimate status surface. Even then, Washington did not move aggressively to create a strong political entity there, concentrating instead on using it as a base for unseating Saddam.

Provide Comfort had several unanticipated long-term effects. Most important, it created stakes where none existed before. Once the United States decided to act for humanitarian reasons and to reassure Turkey, it became committed to the existence of this enclave in the eyes of the Kurds, Saddam, and many people in the United States, despite carefully worded administration statements that avoided an explicit security guarantee. Thus, when Saddam attacked the enclave in 1996, U.S. credibility was on the line.

The United States also was forced to depend on unreliable partners—the Kurds. Neither of the two main Kurdish factions fit U.S. criteria for an attractive partner. The Kurds regularly fought among themselves and often attacked Iraqi forces without U.S. approval. U.S. analysts did not expect peace to last among the Kurds—and it did not—but no alternative existed to them when the inevitable infighting occurred. The diplomatic sensitivities that contributed to a de facto rather than de jure protectorate also led Washington to avoid measures that would create a strong Kurdish political entity in the north.

ESTABLISHING A SOUTHERN NO-FLY ZONE (AUGUST 1992–PRESENT)

The United States and its allies established the southern no-fly zone in August 1992, following brutal attacks by Iraqi forces on the Shi'a population in southern Iraq. Like the Kurds, the Shi'a had risen up following the end of Desert Storm.[5] And as he had done with the Kurds, Saddam brutally suppressed these revolts. The decision to protect the Shi'a, however, took far longer to reach. As noted above, many U.S. policymakers believed that support for the Shi'a would assist Iran, which was then seen in Washington as the leading threat to U.S. interests in the region. The suffering of the Shi'a received far less media coverage than did that of the Kurds, reducing pressure on Western policymakers to act.

The United States organized a limited coalition to support and participate in enforcement operations of a declared zone below the thirty-second parallel. U.S. officials justified this operation, dubbed "Southern Watch," under UN Security Council Resolution 688 which prohibited the Iraqi government from repressing its own people. Most of the air assets used to enforce Southern Watch flew from bases in the Persian Gulf, particularly in Saudi Arabia.

Military action was limited to enforcing a no-fly zone, a relatively easy task given the weakness of the Iraqi Air Force and its limited air-defense network. The United States did not deploy any ground troops to stop the killings or otherwise try to create protected havens for refugees, as it did in Operation Provide Comfort. Neither did the United States commit to military action against Iraqi troops, tanks, artillery, and other ground forces even though at the time Iraq kept eight to ten divisions (perhaps as many as 60,000 troops) in southern Iraq.

---

[5]The scope of the Shi'a rebellions and their initial success were far more limited than were those of the Kurds. Shi'a uprisings achieved success in only seven Iraqi cities and had little support in the countryside. Several Shi'a tribes actually fought on behalf of the Baath regime.

U.S. Objectives. The immediate objective, and the one U.S. officials expressed most vocally in public, was to stop air attacks on the Iraqi Shi'a population. Humanitarian advocates had protested a double standard given the active coalition protection of the Kurds. The success of the no-fly zone in stopping the repression in the north led policymakers to hope that a similar effort would stop repression in the south.

This immediate objective was linked to broader efforts to undermine Saddam's regime. President Bush, explaining the U.S. initiative, declared at a news conference, "We continue to look forward to working with a new leadership in Iraq, one that does not brutally suppress its own people." (Albright, 1992.) At the time, several U.S. leaders worried that the United States had not made it clear to potential coup plotters that it truly sought the end of Saddam's regime. A Pentagon official noted that, via southern no-fly zone enforcement operations, the United States hoped to accomplish an "ancillary" benefit of weakening Saddam's leadership, encouraging a military coup by demonstrating his lack of control over parts of the country (Lancaster, 1992). These broader efforts would be furthered by sustaining the Shiite resistance and demonstrating Saddam's military impotence in the eyes of his armed forces.

The no-fly zone over southern Iraq also served an important purpose in containing Iraqi aggression. By maintaining a large air presence in Saudi Arabia and other Gulf states, Washington had a strong capability to strike any Iraqi forces that deployed near Kuwait or Saudi Arabia.

In incorporating the no-fly zone operations into broader U.S. efforts to contain and pressure Iraq, a negative objective—to avoid causing the dismemberment of the country—also guided U.S. policy, much as it had in the northern Iraq crisis. President Bush went out of his way to emphasize publicly that intention: "We seek Iraq's compliance, not its partition. . . . The United States continues to support Iraq's territorial unity and bears no ill will towards its people." (Lancaster, 1992.) The United States and most U.S. regional partners feared a Shi'a rebellion as well as potential regional instability resulting from any fragmentation of Iraq.

Iraqi Objectives. Saddam's objectives were similar to those in the north, but the stakes were higher for him in the south and his position was stronger. In contrast to the Kurdish north, which at various times in Iraq's recent history was not under central government control, retaining control over southern Iraq was essential. The majority of Iraq's population is Shi'a, and if they successfully organized they would pose a far graver threat to Saddam's rule than would the Kurds. Moreover, Saddam's position was stronger by the time the southern no-fly zone was established. Saddam had already consolidated his control over the south and had clearly survived the post–Desert Storm resentment he had unleashed. Because the United States did not deploy ground troops to the south as it did in the north during Provide Comfort, Saddam was not presented with an immediate threat that would lead him to remove his forces.

Saddam did not withdraw his troops and allow the Shi'a de facto sovereignty, as he did the Kurds. Instead, he used ground forces and intelligence services to brutally uproot any suspected pockets of dissent. Under his direction, regime engineers changed the basic hydrography of the region, draining the large swampy areas of the south where rebels hid, even though these swamps had sustained local populations for thousands of years.

Diplomatic Support. Western and regional partners provided varying levels of support for the southern no-fly zone. France and Britain contributed small numbers of combat aircraft to enforcement operations. Saudi Arabia and Kuwait furnished bases. Saudi Arabia, while avoiding public declarations of support, also assisted Southern Watch operations by providing in-flight refueling and reconnaissance and even by flying several patrol sorties (Murphy, 1992). While regional partners supported enforcement operations, their concern about potential instability resulting from fragmentation or an emboldened Shiite insurgency contributed to the U.S. decision to limit the scope and intensity of its military operations and contingency plans. Iraq threatened its Arab neighbors with reprisals if they helped impose the no-fly zone, apparently in an attempt to undermine the coalition, though such threats were never carried out.

Outcome. The most immediate and superficial objective—stopping Iraqi military flights in the southern region—was quickly achieved. Repression, however, continued unabated. As many as 60,000 Shi'a died as Saddam consolidated his control over southern Iraq from 1991–1995. The operation did succeed politically, however, by relieving pressure on U.S. policymakers to act, even if it failed to protect the Iraqi Shi'a.

On numerous occasions since 1992, Iraq has tested the U.S.-led coalition by violating the no-fly zone restrictions, though until the end of 1998, Southern Watch operations generally deterred Iraqi military actions. These provocations were mostly limited, and the exceptions are discussed below.

In the longer term, there is scant evidence that no-fly zone enforcement in the south has undermined the Iraqi regime. It did not significantly assist the Shi'a in resisting Saddam, and the humiliation inflicted appears limited, particularly as Saddam's forces clearly dominated the south in contrast to the north.

The no-fly zone's biggest success has been as an adjunct to containment. The no-fly zone assets provided the coalition with a strong capacity to deter Iraq and strike Iraqi assets for later coercive threats. Particularly after it was augmented with a "no-drive" zone, which limited where Iraq could deploy its heavy forces, it has helped coalition forces prevent Saddam from massing his troops.

Assessment.   One major assumption guiding U.S. policy—that the Shi'a would be a source of greater influence for Iran if they gained power—was probably mistaken. A Shi'a-led Iraq probably would not be an Iranian pawn. Indeed, rivalry between the two states would likely continue, and perhaps even grow. Iraqi Shi'a fought bitterly against the Iranian regime during the Iran-Iraq war; it would be a mistake to expect them to blindly follow Ayatollah Ruhollah Khomeini's lesser successors. Ethnic divisions between Iraqi Arabs and Persians, and Iran's economic problems, also diminish Iraqi Shi'a ardor for Iranian leadership. In fact, Iraq would probably become a rival for the mantle of Shi'a leadership, further reducing Iran's influence among its co-religionists.[6]

---

[6]See Byman (1999a) and Byman (1996) for a more complete discussion of this argument.

The southern no-fly zone was created almost entirely for domestic political reasons, and by that measure it was clearly a success. It helped sustain domestic support for the U.S. presence in the region, by portraying Washington as on the side of the angels. As with the northern no-fly zone, however, the United States created stakes where none existed before. Preserving the no-fly zone became a basic part of containment, even though its utility for protecting Iraqi Shi'a was limited.

RESPONDING TO INSPECTION AND NO-FLY ZONE STANDOFFS (DECEMBER 1992–JANUARY 1993)

In December 1992, Iraq initiated a crisis with coalition forces, making limited incursions in the southern no-fly zone and threatening to shoot down U.S. monitoring aircraft. At roughly the same time, Iraq blocked the inspection of suspected NBC sites.

To coerce Baghdad to stop these provocations, U.S., British, and French forces conducted air strikes against several military sites. On January 13, allied warplanes bombed, among other things, air-defense facilities in the southern no-fly zone. Several days later, the United States struck the Zaa'faraniyah nuclear complex outside of Baghdad with several dozen cruise missiles. The following day, allied aircraft again attacked Iraqi military facilities in the no-fly zones.

During the course of this crisis, Saddam repeatedly offered partial compliance or conditional compliance (for example, Iraq offered to allow inspection flights into the country but only if UN planes stayed out of the southern no-fly zone). At one point, Iraq offered what it termed a "cease-fire" in an apparent attempt to divide the coalition. Such efforts confronted the allies with the following dilemma: because Iraq was at least in partial compliance with weapons inspections and other demilitarization requirements, a robust military response might require sacrificing some of these gains.

In the end, however, Iraq backed down. U.S. and allied military strikes against Iraq in January 1993 compelled Iraq to cease violating the no-fly zones and actively challenging UNSCOM inspections for several years.

U.S. Objectives.   In contrast to the above attempts at coercion, in January 1993 the United States simply wanted to restore the status quo ante in response to Iraqi provocations.   In addition, while the Iraqi provocations themselves posed relatively little direct and immediate threat to U.S. interests, they appeared aimed at testing coalition resolve.   The U.S.-led coercive strikes were therefore aimed at shoring up the credibility of U.S. policy.

Iraqi Objectives.   Iraq's reasoning for challenging UNSCOM and the no-fly zones at this time is not clear.   Western analysts suspected Saddam might have been seeking to test coalition resolve.   At the time, he also faced growing discontent among groups in his power base, suggesting that he sought to score a visible victory by defying the United States.   He also may have sought to focus attention on Iraq, motivated, as he was in subsequent crises, by the belief that sanctions and isolation would continue indefinitely unless he forced their termination by calling worldwide attention to Iraq.

Diplomatic Support.   Britain and France supported the initial military strikes.   Both countries took part in the attacks on air defenses in the no-fly zones.   Paris, however, distanced itself from the subsequent cruise missile strikes.   French diplomats and government spokesmen described the strike as exceeding the scope of UN Security Council resolutions and said any action against Iraq should be "appropriate and proportionate." (Buchan, 1993; Lewis, 1993.)

U.S., British, and French strikes generated widespread opposition among regional partners and major powers—enough to give rise to speculation that Saddam had deliberately incited U.S. reprisals to win Arab support for lifting of sanctions (Fineman, 1993a).   Arab states, fearing public backlash in response to U.S. military action against a regional power, urged Washington to call off further strikes (Robinson, 1993).   A former Egyptian Ambassador to the United States urged "a pause from the policy of military escalation against Iraq in order to stop the rapid erosion of favorable Arab public opinion, which was the base of support for allied action against Saddam Hussein in the Gulf War." (El Reedy, 1993.)   Turkey also worried that an extended conflict could contribute to its own Kurdish crisis, and Russia, under pressure from nationalist hardliners eager to reestablish economic ties with Iraq, criticized the U.S. air strikes.   Civilian casualties resulting from an errant cruise missile that hit a Baghdad hotel fueled this dissent.[7]

These concerns by other states restricted the range of aggressive actions considered by U.S. decisionmakers (Wright, 1993). The United States avoided heavier air strikes or ones on targets beyond air-defense or NBC sites. In part because of allied resistance and in part because Iraqi provocations were not viewed as extreme, Washington held itself to what it viewed as proportionate responses. Critics of the U.S. action saw it as wavering and ineffectual and recommended more robust, sustained military action, especially against assets of Saddam's elite units (in the hope that such attacks would increase the probability of a coup) (Healy, 1993).

Outcomes. Following the U.S.-led military strikes, Iraq did not openly defy UNSCOM (though the deception campaign continued) and avoided provocations of the no-fly zone for several years. Coalition unity, however, began to fracture, scoring a notable success for Iraq. U.S. credibility also may have been diminished in Iraq's eyes. The weak nature of the strikes, and the immediate criticism by France and various Arab allies of follow-on strikes on Zaa'faraniyah, may have emboldened Saddam for future provocations.

Assessment. From an analytical standpoint, the nature of this crisis and U.S. demands differed considerably from the previous cases discussed. The United States had its policies, instruments, and supporting diplomatic and military structure already in place. It sought to protect them, rather than to impose new ones.

Given the extremely limited nature of the U.S. attacks, Iraq's temporary compliance was surprising. This compliance suggests that Saddam may have feared damage to Iraq's NBC sites, more air strikes if his provocations continued, or disenchantment among his core followers stemming from his engagement in a campaign he could not win. It also may reflect the fact that some of his objectives were achieved anyway.

---

[7]For example, the Arab League issued a statement following the incident that it "regrets the policy of military escalation against Iraq" and further complained that U.S. military action "extended to the bombing of Iraqi civilian targets inside Baghdad and led to the killing and wounding of civilians among the brotherly Iraqi people." (Gordon, 1993.)

The tension between coalition unity and credibility also became apparent in the 1993 strikes. To preserve the coalition, the United States limited its attacks, and even then criticism grew. The weak attacks, however, possibly further diminished U.S. credibility, making Saddam more likely to challenge the United States in the future.

DETERRING AN INVASION OF KUWAIT (1994)

On October 5, 1994, intelligence analysts discovered Iraq was deploying two Republican Guard armored divisions near the Iraq-Kuwait border. Iraq made bellicose statements regarding Kuwait and also threatened to expel UNSCOM inspectors.

The United States responded by rapidly deploying troops to the theater (Operation Vigilant Warrior) and threatening large-scale strikes if Iraq did not withdraw. On October 15, the UN Security Council passed resolution 949, which demanded that Iraq pull back its forces and that Iraq not again deploy its forces near the Kuwaiti border. Both the United States and Britain subsequently warned Iraq that they would use force to stop any Iraqi buildup south of the thirty-second parallel (Herr, 1996, p. 33).

Vigilant Warrior was a massive effort. Already, U.S.-led coalition forces had a substantial air presence in the region to enforce Operation Southern Watch. To reinforce this presence, the United States sent the aircraft carrier *George Washington* to the region, moved additional strike and reconnaissance assets there, dispatched a Marine Corps Expeditionary Unit, and sent an Army Mechanized Task Force. The United States also deployed additional air assets, while the French sent a destroyer, and the British a frigate and destroyer (Herr, 1996, pp. 27–29).

After this rapid buildup, Saddam announced on October 10 that his forces would withdraw. Iraq pulled back its forces from the border area and recognized both Kuwait's sovereignty and the Iraq-Kuwait border. Perhaps fearing that domestic discontent or unrest among the military might spread as a result, Saddam on October 7 established yet another regime protection force, the Fedayeen Saddam, to preserve regime stability.

U.S. Objectives. The United States sought to prevent any Iraqi attack on Kuwait and Saudi Arabia. Equally important, Washington sought to signal its allies that it would defend their territory against any aggression. A strong buildup would demonstrate to both Saddam and to U.S. allies U.S. capabilities and commitment.

Iraqi Objectives. Several motivations probably drove Saddam. High-level defector reporting later indicated that Saddam was considering another cross-border attack if there was no U.S. response (*Al-Watan*, 1995). Saddam may, however, have simply decided to call attention to the region, trying to bully Kuwait to have sanctions removed. The Iraqi dictator may also have been trying to prove to core supporters at home that he could defy the United States (Crosette, 1994; Melloan, 1994; Sciolino, 1994; Byman, 1999b). The timing of the provocations suggests the importance of domestic motives: the Iraqi dinar was plummeting, forcing Saddam to increase food prices and otherwise making his regime unpopular (Baram, 1998, p. 79).

Diplomatic Support. Allies in Europe and elsewhere did not share the U.S. alarm. Even though they contributed to Vigilant Warrior, French officials saw U.S. domestic politics, not an Iraqi threat, as motivating the massive U.S. deployment (Drozdiak, 1994). China and Russia accepted the U.S. decision to send troops, though not enthusiastically (Herr, 1996, p. 37).

Allies in the region supported the deployment initially, but their support waned over time. Saudi Arabia and Kuwait accepted the massive influx of U.S. troops. Once Iraq withdrew, however, several allies complained privately about what they saw as a U.S. overreaction. As these allies faced domestic criticism for their close ties to Washington, the extensive and highly visible U.S. buildup imposed political costs on them.

Outcomes. Vigilant Warrior and its aftermath were largely a coercion victory for the United States and its allies. Not only was an Iraqi invasion deterred, but Resolution 949 laid the groundwork for "red lines" that have since made a surprise attack far less likely. Iraq's subsequent recognition of the Iraq-Kuwait border and of Kuwait's independence both were important U.S. demands.

The U.S. response to the Iraqi provocation, however, proved a political strain on U.S. allies in the region and costly for the United States. This strain made allies more reluctant both to host similar U.S. surges and to identify closely with the United States. The source of such pressures had little to do with U.S. operations, but the U.S. deployment was a focal point for critics. The cost of the operation, and the lack of any apparent penalty to Saddam, also led critics in the United States to charge that Saddam could force Washington to engage in an expensive surge operation with no cost to himself.

Assessment. The long-term outcome of the crisis has strongly favored the United States. Saddam has not engaged in a major troop movement near Kuwait since Vigilant Warrior. The speed of the U.S. deployment appears to have profoundly impressed the Iraqi leadership. This has not prevented Iraqi provocations, but it has changed their size and nature considerably.

If Iraq's moves were motivated by a desire to end sanctions or to shore up prestige at home, they backfired. Dissatisfaction with sanctions at the UN was growing before Saddam made his move, but his aggression helped Washington maintain the international consensus on sanctions. As Pakistan's UN Ambassador noted, "Every time lifting the sanctions comes up, the Iraqis do something to ensure that sanctions will not be lifted."[8] Similarly, Saddam's concessions regarding Kuwait and his rapid drawdown suggest that he might have lost face among supporters at home. The Iraqi leader's decision to create the Fedayeen Saddam also suggests his concern that his retreat would have costs at home.

The political costs of the operation with U.S. regional allies, however, has ironic policy implications for *deterrence*: when deterrence succeeds, its success is often difficult to prove—who knows, for sure, if Saddam really would have invaded Kuwait again? As a result, successful deterrence strategies, such as Vigilant Warrior, are often criticized as costly overreactions, even by the parties who benefited most. Though Vigilant Warrior clearly was a short-term success, it nevertheless had limited negative long-term ramifications for U.S. Gulf security goals.

---

[8]Quoted in Herr (1996, p. 17).

Iraq's true intentions with regard to Kuwait's independence are also questionable. Iraqi Vice President Taha Yasin Ramadan implicitly questioned Iraq's commitment when he noted that the new border has "no judicial value." Most Iraqis seem to believe that a Baath-led Iraq would again try to conquer Kuwait (Baram, 1998, p. 138). The Iraqi guarantee, on its own, is worth little.

The Clinton administration briefly considered, and quickly rejected, conducting strikes against Iraqi forces to punish Baghdad for threatening Kuwait. Given the cost of transporting thousands of U.S. personnel and assets to defend against a possible Iraqi attack and a desire to send a strong message to Saddam to refrain from threatening his neighbors, decisionmakers considered strikes against Iraqi assets. The additional costs of these strikes, however, and a fear of a negative reaction from regional allies dissuaded decisionmakers from taking further action.

PUNISHING THE IRAQI THRUST INTO NORTHERN IRAQ (1996)

After months of growing strife, open warfare erupted between the two leading Kurdish factions—the Kurdish Democratic Party (KDP) and the Patriotic Union of Kurdistan (PUK)—in northern Iraq, a zone under an ambiguous level of protection by the United States. The PUK, with help from Iran, appeared to gain the upper hand. To avoid defeat, the KDP called on Iraq to help repel the PUK. On August 29, Saddam moved into northern Iraq, the area his government had earlier assumed was under U.S. protection, with 30,000–40,000 troops and thousands more police and intelligence personnel, along with several hundred tanks and artillery pieces (Gunter, 1996; Deutch, 1996). Iraqi troops took much of the north, including the Kurdish-held city of Irbil. In addition, Iraqi security forces rounded up hundreds of opposition members and supporters, executing and imprisoning them. Thousands more were evacuated to the United States.

Although the United States did not have a formal commitment to ensuring the security of the Kurdish enclave under Security Council Resolution 688, Washington's previous actions appeared to commit it to ensuring that the Iraqi regime respect the Kurds' human rights, a commitment challenged by the Iraqi attacks. Iraq's previous reaction to the establishment of a protected area in northern Iraq strongly hints that Saddam *perceived* the area as under U.S. protection. Indeed, the United States had even warned the Iraqis twice in the week before the invasion not to interfere in the factional conflict (Riedel, 1996).

In response to Saddam's attack, the United States launched 44 cruise missiles at fixed, above-ground targets in southern Iraq, primarily surface-to-air missile (SAM) sites, radar installations, and command and control facilities (Operation Desert Strike). In addition to the cruise missile attacks, the United States extended the no-fly zone in the south, which before had ended at the thirty-second parallel, to the thirty-third parallel. The zone's extension was intended to further limit Iraq's ability to move its forces and to improve the U.S.-led coalition's ability to monitor the regime (Riedel, 1996).

Saddam responded quickly to the limited U.S. attack. Iraq had concentrated forces near Chamchamal, a Kurdish-held city en route to the PUK's base at Sulaymaniyah. After the strikes, Saddam dispersed the Republican Guard and pulled his forces back to the cease-fire line.

U.S. Objectives. U.S. objectives in response to the Iraqi incursion were to avoid the appearance of weakness while maintaining the support of U.S. allies, who generally opposed the strikes. Ostensibly, the strikes were linked to overall U.S. efforts to defend the Kurds, but administration and military officials barely paid lip service to this goal. The strikes in the south also were intended to convince Saddam to pull back, though U.S officials were not optimistic that they would succeed (Deutch, 1996). Thus, the more modest goal of the strikes was to punish Saddam for his aggression, demonstrating there was a price to be paid for blatant provocations. This punishment, U.S. officials hoped, would help maintain U.S. credibility in the region.

Washington also sought to preserve the stability of U.S. allies, which might be damaged by a stronger U.S. strike. The Iraqi incursion came shortly after the June 25, 1996, Khobar Towers attack, where terrorists killed 19 U.S. servicemen in Saudi Arabia. At this sensitive time, the United States did not want to give more ammunition to the

Saudi regime's critics, who opposed the U.S. regional presence and regular strikes on Iraq.

Iraqi Objectives. Striking a blow against the Kurdish opposition in the face of perceived U.S. resistance helped Saddam restore his damaged prestige at home. The existence of, and activities within, the northern protected zone threatened Saddam's relationship with his power base. In March 1996, Kurdish forces teamed up with soldiers of the Iraqi National Congress, defeating Iraqi forces in a minor skirmish. Although the damage done to regime forces was limited, it humiliated Saddam and increased criticism within his power base. In the months before the attack, several of Saddam's family members defected, tribal tension increased, and members of the security services attempted a coup (Baram, 1998, p. 4). By challenging what most Iraqis perceived as a U.S. protectorate, Saddam demonstrated to his core supporters that he remained capable of defying the United States. Saddam also demonstrated to all Iraqis, both supporters and opponents, that he was a force to be reckoned with inside Iraq's borders. The incursion in the north also gave the Iraqi military a much-needed victory after years of defeat and humiliation. Iraqi officials proclaimed that Iraq's flag "flies high" and the American flag flies "at half-staff."[9]

A victory against the opposition also enabled Saddam to make concessions on other issues. Sanctions were taking a bite and would soon force Saddam to accept the oil-for-food deal, which he long opposed. By invading the north, Saddam proved his mettle and was thus better able to yield on other fronts (Baram, 1998, p. 51).

Diplomatic Support. Neither the regional nor the Western allies of the United States showed support for even token operations against Iraq on behalf of the Kurds. Arab allies had little sympathy for the fate of the Kurds. Saudi Arabia feared that helping the PUK against Saddam would strengthen Iran's influence over Iraq.[10] In general, regional governments viewed Saddam's involvement in the Kurdish

---

[9]Quoted in Baram (1998, p. 51).

[10]Concern with even a tacit alliance with Iran also limited U.S. options. Sens. John Warner and Strom Thurmond, in open hearings, both expressed concern that U.S. intervention in the north would place the United States on the same side as Tehran (Baker, 1996).

civil war as an internal Iraqi matter, not one that required U.S. intervention. Several allies, particularly Egypt, noted that no UN resolution prevented Iraqi forces from acting in any part of Iraq (*Al-Sharq*, 1996b). Arab regimes feared that U.S. strikes would fuel dissent at home.

The Turkish government opposed the U.S. military operation though its opposition was neither strong nor highly vocal. The Turkish General Staff was concentrating on destroying Turkey's own Kurdish insurgency and feared any actions that helped the Kurds (Deutch, 1996). At the time, Turkey was also under the short-lived government of the Islamist-oriented Refah party, which was more inclined toward improving Turkish-Iraqi relations (Ergin, 1996).

This lack of regional support severely constrained the U.S. use of threats and force. Riyadh and Ankara withheld access to bases in their countries for Desert Strike, preventing a prompt and massive U.S. response (Haass, 1996; Cordesman, 1996). The limits imposed by Turkey, Jordan, and Saudi Arabia made the use of large numbers of land-based fighters impossible. Because of range limits, carrier-based aircraft from the Gulf also were not available for strikes in northern Iraq (Horner, 1996). Saudi Arabia and other states did, however, support the extension of the no-fly zone (Riedel, 1996; Kremp, 1996).

Other major powers also criticized U.S. actions. Russia openly criticized the U.S. strikes and quashed a British-sponsored Security Council resolution that condemned Iraqi military action against the Kurds (Deutch, 1996, Interfax, 1996). In the UN Security Council, Russia and China refused to condemn Saddam's actions and openly criticized the U.S. strike (Kremp, 1996; Beijing Central, 1996). Spain refused to allow the United States access to its air bases for F-117A fighters destined for Iraq, even though the Spanish government publicly supported the U.S. attacks (Gonzalez and Cembrero, 1996).[11] Japan and Germany voiced support for the attacks, but their support appeared perfunctory. Several Arab and European newspapers attributed the strikes to President Clinton's electoral needs (*Al-Sharq*, 1996a; Kremp, 1996; Beijing Central, 1996).

---

[11]The stopover in Moron de la Frontera was not necessary, but it was standard practice for aircraft.

France tried to straddle the fence, working with the United States while attempting to distance itself from U.S. actions. The French joined the United States and Britain in warning Iraq that it would protect the no-fly zone and coalition pilots, but it appears that this warning was the most Washington and London could gain: Paris refused any stronger threat or harsher language (Miller, 1996). France also criticized the U.S. strikes in the UN Security Council.

Outcomes. Saddam pulled back his forces from northern Iraq following the U.S. strikes. Nevertheless, the Iraqi incursion into the Kurdish zone was a major blow to U.S. prestige and strengthened Saddam's position at home. Although U.S. policymakers had carefully avoided any explicit commitment to protecting the Kurds, previous statements threatening Saddam and the considerable U.S. diplomatic and intelligence presence in the north, combined with the Baath's previous respect for the zone, put U.S. prestige on the line. Saddam's domestic position grew far stronger as a result of his forays into the north: his operations shattered the U.S.-backed opposition and enhanced Saddam's standing with the army and other core supporters (Eisenstadt, 1996). Then–CIA Director John Deutch admitted that Saddam's actions had bolstered his regional prestige (Deutch, 1996).

As a result of Saddam's incursion, the Iraqi opposition was largely destroyed as a fighting force, setting back U.S. aspirations of changing the regime in Baghdad. Saddam became a major power broker among the Kurds, demonstrating that he retains influence in the region and that the local balance of power depends on his acquiescence.

Saddam probably believed he had successfully split the coalition. The Iraqi press praised Russia, and also noted that France's position indicated that it did not support Washington (Iraqi News Agency, 1996). In the past, Paris had strongly supported Operation Provide Comfort while in this instance it clearly had abandoned the Kurds.

Assessment. The United States weighed a range of military responses before choosing the more limited Desert Strike plan. In the end, decisionmakers chose not to bomb military targets near Baghdad nor forces in northern Iraq—a decision widely criticized by former government officials and other analysts (Baker, 1996).[12] Limits on basing prevented a sustained strike on targets in northern Iraq. Attacking targets in the north with naval air assets would have required refueling above Iraqi territory, which would have left U.S. aircraft vulnerable to Iraqi antiaircraft assets. Cruise missiles were poorly suited for the mission.[13] Casualty sensitivity also limited U.S. options. Sending nonstealthy aircraft to attack Baghdad, for example, was deemed too risky to U.S. airmen (Horner, 1996). A limited response also was in line with U.S. political strategy. Saddam's forces withdrew from northern Iraq, and neighbors were not threatened, thus fulfilling the basic goals of containment.

The destruction of targets in the south did little actual damage to Saddam, but his response suggests a sensitivity to air strikes. The targets destroyed mattered only if a larger attack were being considered, as air-defense sites themselves are not an instrument of control or other means of leverage (Perle, 1996). Saddam's risk-averse response to the strikes is surprising in light of the moderate immediate costs of resistance. Saddam's abandonment of the attack on Chamchamal lessened the scope of his victory. By dispersing the Republican Guard Saddam also reminded his forces that Iraq had no counter to U.S. air strikes. They had to hide, not retaliate. Equally important, dispersing the Guard lessened his ability to prevent a coup, because it removed one obstacle to a seizure of power.

U.S. setbacks stemmed from diplomatic failures, both in the region and among Iraqi opposition groups. Saddam seized an opportunity, he did not engineer it. The United States failed to maintain unity among the opposition groups. Opposition infighting was foreseeable, as the Kurds had a history of internecine warfare. Indeed, Kurdish infighting began in May 1994 and continued in the following months, ample time for the United States to recognize the magnitude of the problem and to intervene. Saddam exploited this infighting, as he had in the past, to consolidate his control.

---

[12]The United States had also agreed to, but not implemented, the oil-for-food arrangement. Critics of U.S. policy called for canceling the arrangement to punish Saddam's provocations (Perle, 1996).

[13]Using cruise missiles against mobile forces, such as Iraqi armor, is difficult because they require advanced programming (Horner, 1996).

The United States also failed to recognize the extent of its commitment to northern Iraq and to plan accordingly. As a result, when Saddam's assault came, the United States lacked the support of states in the region for a muscular response. None of the regional states supported a strong U.S. response and, of the major powers, only Britain actually backed U.S. actions. This lack of support hindered an effective military response.

The crisis also disproved one of the assumptions the United States had about its Kurdish allies. Analysts and policymakers assumed that the Iraqi Kurds had nowhere to turn for assistance other than the United States (Cockburn and Cockburn, 1999, p. 236). They ignored the Kurds' history of forming alliances of convenience with both Iran and with the regime in Baghdad as a means to ascendancy over their rivals within the Kurdish community.

HALTING DEFIANCE OF UNSCOM (1997–1998)

From autumn 1997 through the end of 1998, Saddam blocked UNSCOM inspections on numerous occasions, leading the United States to issue coercive threats in several instances. This confrontation probably would have come sooner, had it not been for the August 1995 defection of Husayn Kamil, which panicked the regime and led it to reveal considerable material on its NBC programs. Even so, throughout 1996, Iraq constantly blocked inspectors from entering suspected NBC sites, harassed them, and otherwise prevented UNSCOM from completing its mission.

The initial UN response to this interference was tepid at best. On October 6, 1997, the chief of UNSCOM, Richard Butler, reported that Iraq's account of its biological programs was not remotely credible and that Iraq was systematically interfering with the inspectors' work. Despite this report, the Security Council refused to authorize the use of force against Iraq in response. The Security Council blocked U.S. and British proposals to threaten Iraq with military strikes or otherwise ratchet up pressure. This weak response apparently emboldened Saddam.

On October 29, 1997, Iraq announced its intention to expel American members of the inspection teams and later threatened to shoot down U-2 spy planes monitoring Iraqi compliance. The United States responded by increasing it military forces in the region and threatening strikes if Iraq did not comply. Following the U.S. buildup, Iraq rescinded its ultimatums and readmitted the expelled inspectors. Baghdad then announced that Saddam's presidential palaces would be off-limits. After the United States again moved to the brink of military strikes, on February 23, 1998, UN Secretary General Kofi Annan brokered a deal ending Saddam's opposition to inspections in return for several concessions that greatly weakened the inspection effort.

Although the Annan deal bought several months of inspections without a standoff, in August 1998 Iraq protested continued sanctions and announced its intention to end its relationship with inspectors. At the end of October it blocked UN monitoring efforts. The United States and Britain threatened military strikes to coerce Iraqi compliance. After the UN withdrew much of its staff in November, the United States launched B-52 bombers to attack Iraq. Having been criticized at home for "pinprick" strikes on Iraq in 1996, the Clinton administration and the military prepared for more extensive strikes on Iraq. At the last minute, Saddam agreed to submit to the inspections once again, and the strikes were called off.

U.S. Objectives. The United States and its allies sought to coerce Iraqi compliance with the UNSCOM inspection and monitoring regime while maintaining coalition unity. U.S. policymakers were in a constant battle between diplomatic feasibility and effective inspections. The United States sought to keep a united front against Iraq in the face of growing opposition to both sanctions and inspections. Thus, they agreed to compromises that made the inspections less effective, leading to charges that they supported "the illusion of arms control."

Iraqi Objectives. Saddam probably sought to defy UNSCOM to bring about the end of sanctions altogether as well as to preserve his NBC programs. Saddam probably intended to remind the international community to speed the lifting of sanctions and, more important, to demonstrate to his supporters that he remained defiant (Baram, 1998, p. 79). Saddam sought not only to have sanctions lifted but to have this occur in a way that would reinforce his prestige. In essence, he could demonstrate to his power base that the NBC programs they favor remained intact while forcing the end of sanctions.

Diplomatic Support. Initial diplomatic support was limited, but it steadily grew as Iraqi defiance continued even in the face of U.S. and UN concessions. Weariness with constant confrontations, concern about the humanitarian impact of sanctions, and setbacks in the Arab-Israeli peace process had frustrated many Arab leaders with Washington (Telhami, 1997; Grier, 1997). Saudi Arabia and Bahrain even denied the United States access to bases for strikes on Iraq (Cockburn and Cockburn, 1999, pp. 272–275). By the time of the November 1998 standoff, though, Saddam was isolated in the Arab world. The favorable terms of the Annan agreement had led many in the region to anticipate that Iraq would submit to superficial inspections, with the expectations that Baghdad would soon get a clean bill of health. Iraq's open defiance of the already watered-down inspection regime, however, proved too much. As in the past, Saddam proved to be his own worst enemy. Eight Arab states (Egypt, Syria, and the Persian Gulf states) warned that Iraq alone would take the blame for consequences stemming from its defiance, implying that even if they did not endorse military action, they would not strongly oppose it (Crosette, 1998a, 1998b). More to the point, the states of the region provided the necessary basing for the U.S. strike campaign that was hastily called off in November 1998.

Among major powers, grudging support for strikes against Iraq grew. Despite Iraq's repeated interference with inspections and regular UNSCOM reports that several Iraqi programs were not accounted for, members of the international community defected from the anti-Iraq coalition throughout much of 1996 and 1997. Weak international support persisted even after Saddam became blatant in his violations. On October 23, 1997, the Security Council passed Resolution 1134, which threatened to restrict the travel of Iraqi officials if Saddam did not comply with inspections. Such a resolution was hardly a coercive hammer, but Russia, China, France, and Egypt all abstained from the vote. In January 1998, Russian President Boris Yeltsin even hinted that U.S. strikes in Iraq might lead to a U.S.-Russian confrontation (Wurmser, 1999, p. 4). As with states in the region, however, Iraq's brazen defiance of token inspections and abrogation of the Annan agreement led the major powers to support, or at least not strongly oppose, U.S. strikes in November.

Outcomes. In the short term, the threats of military strikes coerced Saddam to retreat and promise to cooperate with UNSCOM. This cooperation, of course, was honored only in the breach. In fact, Saddam may have regarded the showdown as a partial success. He won some significant concessions with respect to the inspection regime, exposed divisions between the United States and its allies, and publicized the suffering of the Iraqi population as a result of continued sanctions. More immediately, inspections, in effect, came to a halt.

The United States managed to preserve the anti-Iraq coalition, but at the price of UNSCOM effectiveness. The Annan agreement effectively neutered UNSCOM, making it little better than a glorified IAEA. Given the initial widespread opposition in the region and among major powers to strikes, however, the consensus Washington built by November 1998 was an impressive achievement, though Saddam deserves much of the credit because he overplayed his hand.

Assessment. Saddam squandered potential gains even while he discredited the United States. Had Saddam simply abided by the terms of the Annan agreement, which essentially limited the extent of inspections, Iraq soon would have met the United Nations' criteria for its NBC programs, paving the way to the lifting of sanctions. Moreover, his October 1997 provocations had exposed rifts in the Security Council, but Saddam failed to understand the balance Paris, Beijing, and Moscow sought to keep with the United States. While they could tolerate a lack of compliance, they could not defend open defiance. Saddam's desire for a dramatic win worked against the interests of his foreign supporters, who needed a humble and superficially compliant Iraq to justify the lifting of sanctions and the abolition of UNSCOM.

The standoffs did, however, lead to significant domestic criticism of the Clinton administration's policy in the region—the first widespread criticism of U.S. policy with regard to Iraq. Lawmakers and pundits criticized the administration's reluctance to use force and inability to muster a solid coalition.[14] As a result of the criticism, political pressure for a stronger response to any Iraqi intransigence grew.

---

[14]On June 22, 1998, the senior Republican leadership in both the Senate and House of Representatives sent a letter to President Clinton noting their concerns about U.S. policy toward Iraq (Congressional Letter, 1998).

FORCING COMPLIANCE WITH UNSCOM (OPERATION DESERT FOX, DECEMBER 1998)

After the last-minute abort order for the November 1998 strikes—and the criticism that accompanied this decision—the United States was prepared to respond quickly after any further Iraqi defiance of UNSCOM. This opportunity came soon. In December 1998, Ambassador Butler issued his report to the Security Council, which declared that Iraq was not meeting its obligations to UNSCOM. Iraq had blocked UNSCOM inspections even though the inspectors' information was dated and the sites chosen were not sensitive.

In response, the United States and Britain began a large-scale, four-day air and cruise missile campaign against Iraqi military targets (Operation Desert Fox). The United States and Britain launched roughly 600 aircraft sorties and 400 cruise missile strikes against approximately 100 targets, including Iraqi intelligence and security forces facilities, presidential palaces, air-defense systems, NBC sites, and economic targets.

Though far more massive than any previous strike in the Gulf since Desert Storm, Desert Fox remained a limited operation. The allied strikes avoided some Iraqi chemical plants (even though one ultimate aim was to destroy NBC capability), fearing that a strike could unleash poisonous plumes and kill Iraqi civilians. The campaign also ended after only four days to avoid adverse political and diplomatic consequences expected to arise if strikes continued during the Muslim holy month of Ramadan.

Saddam remained defiant of UNSCOM, but his reactions to the strikes indicate his concern with protecting his power base. In response to the bombing and overall crisis, Saddam divided Iraq administratively in a manner that would further increase the control of regime loyalists. Saddam also reinforced some areas, such as Basra, that were prone to unrest and executed several officers who might have been considering a coup. He also cracked down on any potential dissent among the Shi'a, executing religious leaders (Matlak, 1999).

U.S. Objectives. The Desert Fox air campaign was not so much a case of coercion as it was a recognition that past coercion efforts had failed and that any campaign should focus on future coercion efforts.

Defense Secretary William S. Cohen articulated the following objectives: "We want to degrade Saddam Husayn's ability to make and to use weapons of mass destruction. We want to diminish his ability to wage war against his neighbors. And we want to demonstrate the consequences of flouting international obligations." (Department of Defense, 1998.)[15] The first two of these objectives were "brute force" ones, insofar as they aimed to physically destroy Iraqi capacity to conduct certain behavior, rather than to persuade it to desist via threats. The third, to demonstrate adverse consequences of flouting obligations, suggests a broad, long-term coercion goal: to bolster the credibility of the U.S. containment policy and other threats directed at Iraq. Concerns about allied stability also affected the campaign. The campaign's duration was limited in part because the holy month of Ramadan was beginning, and in part because Washington feared the effect of long-lasting strikes.

Some of the allied strikes, particularly those aimed at security force and Special Republican Guard facilities, were probably intended to weaken support for Saddam's regime among those who kept Saddam in power. Although they did not declare it publicly as an objective, U.S. decisionmakers hoped that bombing the assets of these forces might inspire them to move against Saddam. Thus, while NBC-related strikes received much of the media attention and were the rhetorical focus of many policymakers, the attacks on regime assets suggest that Washington had coercive goals as well as brute force ones in mind.

Iraqi Objectives. As with his previous defiance of the UN, Saddam probably sought to disrupt the anti-Iraq coalition, freeing himself from sanctions and inspections simultaneously. It is likely that the previous U.S. strike cancellation, and the limited nature of previous attacks, had convinced the Iraqi leader that he could easily withstand the strikes (perhaps even coming out stronger and less-inhibited by inspectors), if they came at all.

---

[15]President Clinton defined U.S. objectives in similar terms, explaining them as "designed to degrade Saddam's capacity to develop and deliver weapons of mass destruction and to degrade his ability to threaten his neighbors. At the same time we are delivering a powerful message to Saddam. If you act recklessly you will pay a heavy price." (Clinton, 1998.)

Diplomatic Support. As in the past, the strongest allied support came from Britain, which participated in the air campaign. Several major U.S. allies in Europe and Asia voiced support but did not participate in the operation. Russia and China protested vehemently, as did such U.S. allies as Egypt and France. Gulf allies' reactions were cautious, and several allies, including Saudi Arabia, limited U.S. strikes from their territory (Jehl, 1998). The timing of the attack led many foreign governments to question whether the attacks were launched to influence the imminent U.S. presidential impeachment vote rather than because of Iraq's actions.

The Gulf states' support for the strikes grew, at least tacitly, following Saddam's reactions to Desert Fox. The Iraqi leader lashed out at the Gulf states that hosted U.S. forces, reducing any inclination the leaders of these states had to sit on the fence. The Arab press as a result became more anti-Saddam than in the past.

Outcomes. Because of limits on NBC strikes due to fears of Iraqi civilian casualties and the difficulty of identifying Iraqi NBC facilities, the strikes only marginally hindered Iraq's NBC programs. The air strikes also severed Iraq's relations with UNSCOM. Little firm evidence exists that the operation bolstered the credibility and strength of U.S. Iraq policy in the region or with other major powers, but the more forceful nature of the strike probably surprised and shook Saddam. Given his subsequent purges and assassinations, the targets chosen appear to have struck a nerve, making him focus on domestic stability.

Assessment. Desert Fox did not lead Iraq to comply with UNSCOM, or even to avoid further provocations. Shortly after the end of Desert Fox, Iraq began challenging U.S. enforcement of the no-fly zones over northern and southern Iraq. Nevertheless, Desert Fox appeared to have shaken Saddam. Saddam's mass arrests in the south and execution of several officers and religious leaders indicated that he feared domestic instability. Desert Fox's strikes on regime support and protection targets demonstrated that Saddam could not defend his core personnel (Matlak, 1999). Perhaps more important, Saddam's reaction to Desert Fox bolstered the anti-Iraq coalition. States in the region strengthened their ties to Washington in response to Saddam's subsequent threats and criticism.

The duration of the campaign reflected the administration's juggling of domestic and allied concerns. On the one hand, decisionmakers sought to avert Congressional criticism of "pinprick" attacks or of a short-lived campaign. On the other hand, the beginning of Ramadan and fears for allied stability led to the campaign's end after only a few days.

THE CHANGING DYNAMICS OF CONFRONTATION

The U.S. and Iraqi actions in the above cases suggest that several key factors that influence the likelihood of successful coercion changed gradually since the end of Desert Storm. The most important was the size of, and immediate threat posed by, U.S. forces in the region. In the aftermath of Desert Storm, the United States had a massive military presence in the region and in Iraq itself. U.S. forces occupied parts of southern Iraq, while Iraq's military was in disarray. The United States could therefore pose a credible and potent military threat while Iraq was extremely vulnerable. As the United States drew down its forces, and as Saddam gradually consolidated his hold on power, this tremendous imbalance diminished.

The attitudes of regional allies also evolved in the years after Desert Storm. Iraq has successfully portrayed itself as a victim in the Arab world. The West, and the United States in particular, is widely viewed as ignoring the plight of the Iraqi people. At the same time, Saddam's continued survival forced a reappraisal among Gulf states. Although all Gulf leaders would prefer Saddam's removal from power, they recognize that he may hold power for years to come and that developing a modus vivendi may be necessary. The Gulf states in general have become more cautious about supporting U.S. military strikes or open confrontation with Iraq.

The geopolitical environment changed even more dramatically than the regional environment. Russia and China shifted from supporters of Desert Storm to critics of sanctions, inspections, military strikes, and other aspects of U.S. policy. France, which as late as 1993 participated in military strikes on Iraq, became a harsh critic of U.S. actions. This shift both constricted U.S. freedom to choose its options and emboldened Iraq, encouraging Saddam to believe that he had potential supporters for his defiance.

ATTEMPTS TO COERCE IRAQ: A SCORECARD

Figures 5.1 and 5.2 present U.S. and Iraqi objectives, by case. As the tables suggest, motives for the various confrontations varied on both sides. The above eight cases of coercion reveal a mixed record when compared with the overall U.S. goals regarding Iraq discussed in Chapter Four: containing Iraq, stopping Iraq's NBC programs, changing the regime, and preventing the spread of instability.

The containment of Iraq has generally succeeded. A robust regional presence, a rapid surge capacity, and a willingness to use limited

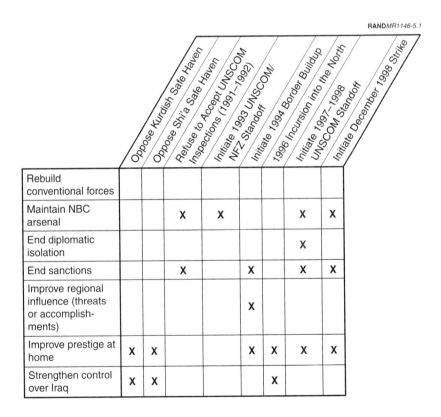

	Oppose Kurdish Safe Haven	Oppose Shi'a Safe Haven	Refuse to Accept UNSCOM Inspections (1991–1992)	Initiate 1993 UNSCOM/NFZ Standoff	Initiate 1994 Border Buildup	1996 Incursion into the North	Initiate 1997–1998 UNSCOM Standoff	Initiate December 1998 Strike
Rebuild conventional forces								
Maintain NBC arsenal			X	X			X	X
End diplomatic isolation							X	
End sanctions			X		X		X	X
Improve regional influence (threats or accomplishments)					X			
Improve prestige at home	X	X			X	X	X	X
Strengthen control over Iraq	X	X				X		

RAND*MR1146-5.1*

Figure 5.1—Saddam's Primary Objectives, by Case

RAND*MR1146-5.2*

	Establish Kurdish Safe Haven	Establish Shi'a Safe Haven	Force Acceptance of UNSCOM Inspections (1991–1992)	1992–1993 UNSCOM/ NFZ Standoff	1994 Border Buildup	1996 Incursion into the North	1997–1998 UNSCOM Standoff	December 1998 Strike
Keep Iraqi conventional forces weak								X
Halt Iraqi NBC programs			X	X			X	X
Remove Saddam from power	X[a]							X
Protect subjugated Iraqi peoples	X	X				X		
Ensure security of Gulf allies (from immediate threat)		X			X			
Minimize U.S. casualties[b]						X		
Maintain sanctions							X	
Prevent destabilization of allies	X				X	X	X	X
Maintain Iraq's diplomatic isolation						X	X	

[a]Removing Saddam from power did not motivate the creation of the northern protective zone, but, once created, this zone was exploited for anti-Saddam activities.

[b]Minimizing U.S. casualties is a high priority for any U.S. military operation. This is listed as a category here for cases when the political leadership sought to prevent any casualties, even if it severely constrained operations.

Figure 5.2—U.S. Objectives That Affected the Use of Force, by Case

force probably have convinced Saddam that regional aggression will not succeed. Saddam Husayn's Iraq is far weaker than it was in 1990, both in relative and in absolute terms. In Richard Haass's words, Iraq today is "better understood as constituting a dangerous nuisance than an actual strategic threat." (Haass, 1996.) In 1996, military analyst Anthony Cordesman estimated that Iraq's military capacity was roughly 20 percent of what it was in 1990 (Cordesman, 1996). Iraq's regional influence, while increased from 1991, remains limited. Coercive threats contributed to containment by maintaining no-fly and no-drive zones, deterring Iraqi aggression, and demonstrating regional unity in the face of Iraq's attempts to intimidate its neighbors.

Stopping Iraq's NBC programs has proven extremely difficult, but coercive threats have achieved some success. Iraq probably has not attained a nuclear weapon, and progress on its biological and chemical programs has probably halted (though data remain scarce)—a clear success when we recognize that without UNSCOM inspections, sanctions, and other measures Iraq would probably have a nuclear weapon and a range of biological weapons. Nevertheless, the broader U.S. goals of discovering the extent of Iraq's programs, destroying them, and preventing Iraq from reconstituting them in the future have not been met. Inspectors never discovered the true scope of Iraq's programs, much less destroyed them. Effective inspections ended in early 1998, and even the pretense of arms control has now been abandoned. Although information is scarce, Saddam is probably trying to continue some programs already and certainly will do so in the future once sanctions and isolation end. While threats of force have persuaded Saddam at various times to accept inspections and uses of force have knocked out some of his NBC program resources, the various U.S. actions have not substantially induced a change in Saddam's long-term policies towards acquiring such an arsenal. Although the current level of NBC infrastructure in Iraq may be limited, the country's scientific and engineering base remains robust and has the capability to rapidly restore NBC programs to past levels should international efforts to prevent these programs wane.

Maximal U.S. goals were not met. Efforts to change the regime—by encouraging Iraqi elites to support a coup or the Iraqi populace to overthrow Saddam—probably are farther from success than at any time this decade. The Iraqi opposition is fragmented. Several Kurdish and Shi'a groups maintain some, but very limited, capacity to operate against Saddam. Saddam's successful weathering of various past coercive threats has increased his stature at home and, as always, the regime vigilantly stamps out any sign of unrest. Coercive threats nevertheless made this goal more realistic. The protected zone in the north and the humiliations of air strikes contributed to discontent among Saddam's followers, though not enough to coerce a successful regime change.

The tendency for commentators to focus on tangible policy results should not obscure that the United States has largely met its negative objective: keeping the region stable. Instability from Iraq has not spread to Turkey or other U.S. allies. Although Islamists and other anti-U.S. oppositionists regularly criticize the United States for its military presence in the Gulf region, the anti-Iraq campaign is only a limited source of their anger and various strikes on Iraq have only marginally increased their resentment (Byman and Green, 1999).[16]

U.S. POLICY TRADEOFFS AND GULF SECURITY

Beyond these findings, a deeper understanding of success or failure requires a counterfactual thought experiment: what would have happened without various U.S. attempts to coerce Iraq? In general, U.S. efforts to coerce Iraq resulted in advances—or prevented dangerous setbacks—for U.S. policy in the region and in general. Without continued U.S. pressure, Iraq would almost certainly have rearmed itself and furthered its NBC programs. Had U.S. pressure ended shortly after Desert Storm, Iraq might have a far more extensive biological program and probably some nuclear capacity. In addition, Iraq probably would have rebuilt its conventional forces, which currently suffer from inadequate equipment in poor repair and from the lack of skilled personnel.

The benefits the United States gained through repeated confrontations with Iraq have carried a price. The large and constant presence has proved draining for the U.S. military, hindering training and straining forces in general. The U.S. presence in the Gulf region has

---

[16]A complete U.S. withdrawal would offset some, but not all, of this criticism. Such a withdrawal, however, is not likely, regardless of which coercive options the United States pursues in the future.

also enraged radical Islamists, who have attacked U.S. facilities in other parts of the world in retaliation. Washington's repeated confrontations also contributed to an intangible but nevertheless widespread stereotype of the United States as an aggressive hegemon. Critics among our Western allies and in Russia, China, and the Muslim world cite U.S. strikes on Iraq as proof that the United States is quick to use force and often acts without the consensus of the international community.

Chapter Six

IRAQ'S VULNERABILITIES: AN ASSESSMENT

The cases examined in Chapter Five reveal that Saddam is sensitive to a variety of pressures, particularly those that threaten his relationship with his power base and prestige at home. The impact of U.S. pressure, however, must be measured relative to the stakes involved for Saddam: the same instrument may produce success in one instance and failure in another because the stakes involved for Saddam are higher in the latter case.

The perceived threats that motivate Saddam's reactions to coercive threats are a product not only of targeting the right vulnerabilities but also products of U.S. and coalition credibility as well. After Desert Storm, even limited threats of force produced a quick response by Saddam. He accepted UN inspectors, evacuated the Kurdish north in 1991, and halted interference with UNSCOM in 1993 to avoid any confrontation, despite the domestic humiliation that probably resulted. As the anti-Iraq coalition weakened, however, Saddam became bolder. In 1996, he reestablished his influence in the north, and, in 1997–1998, he systematically pursued a confrontation with UNSCOM. Saddam considered the weak UN response to the UNSCOM reports of violations as a sign of a rift in the alliance, leading him toward further defiance (Baram, 1998, p. 78).

This chapter examines Iraqi vulnerabilities and sensitivity in greater detail, drawing on the cases in Chapter Five to better inform future coercive strategies. It also notes some seemingly likely vulnerabilities that are not really such. It then examines countermeasures that Saddam uses to minimize Iraq's, and his, vulnerability to U.S. coercion measures. We conclude that precisely because Saddam's relationship to his power base is Iraq's critical pressure point, Saddam is often well-equipped to protect it from U.S. threats.

IRAQI PRESSURE POINTS

Saddam's Iraq is sensitive to a variety of pressures. Saddam is most concerned with ensuring that his power base remains behind the regime. To this end, he will concede to coercive actions that threaten this relationship, but he will remain defiant if he perceives defiance as necessary to its stability. He also respects, grudgingly, military reality and strives to maintain domestic control.

Elite Dissatisfaction. The above coercion cases show that Saddam is most vulnerable when his power base is threatened and most intransigent when concessions would decrease support among his power base. Saddam's primary concerns are domestic, not foreign. Maintaining the support and loyalty of key tribes, Baath party officials, military officers, and other elites is his overriding focus. As Amatzia Baram argues, "Throughout his career . . . whenever Iraq's foreign interests clashed with perceived domestic security interests, the latter always prevailed. Insofar as internal security is concerned, Saddam Husayn has never taken any chances." (Baram, 1998, p. 2.) When Saddam's power base can be effectively targeted, he is more likely to limit his foreign policy challenges. After Operation Desert Storm, Saddam's domestic position was weak, and he feared that another blow from the anti-Iraq coalition would shatter it. His response to subsequent threats and weak strikes in the following years evinced his fear of being discredited after military strikes. These strikes heavily swayed Saddam's decisionmaking even if their operational effects were limited.

Just as sensitivity with regard to his power base drove Saddam to back down in several cases, fear of elite dissatisfaction also helps explain instances when Saddam has refused to back down in the face of U.S. pressure. The most notable instance is Saddam's commitment to NBC programs. Although Saddam's initial defiance on this score may be explained by his belief that deception would triumph over UNSCOM and that sanctions would soon be lifted in any event, over time the possession of NBC has become an issue of prestige for Saddam with his core supporters. By publicly defying the United States and its allies over this issue, Saddam has further increased the importance of this issue among key elites. In 1996, he risked defying what he saw as a U.S. security guarantee to score points with the military and nationalists at home. These examples expose a key implication for designing coercion strategies: those measures that demand behavior that would risk an anti-Saddam backlash among his core supporters are likely to fail unless they also threaten to impose an even greater risk of a backlash if Saddam does not comply.

Although—indeed because—it is such a sensitive point, elite dissatisfaction is probably the danger Saddam is most prepared to combat. The very structure of his governing apparatus is centered on preserving power against a coup by members of the armed forces, Baath party, or security services. Although dissatisfaction is widespread and coup attempts occur periodically, Saddam's longevity is testimony to his skill in maintaining himself in power. This focus, however, highlights Saddam's paramount concern for this issue.

Popular Instability. Saddam is somewhat sensitive to the threat of popular unrest. This sensitivity is largely indirect, though, and arises mostly when unrest risks discrediting him with his power base. Saddam is committed to firm control over Iraq, with his Sunni Arab nationalist brand of chauvinism dominant. The predecessors to the Baath government fell in part because they failed to achieve peace at home. Moreover, as Saddam has portrayed himself as the defender of Iraq's integrity (and Sunni Arab hegemony), continued Shi'a, Kurdish, and tribal unrest undercut this source of strength. To weaken the opposition, he risked invading northern Iraq in 1996 despite his fear of a strong U.S. military response.

Until popular opinion affects his relationship with his power base, Saddam generally remains unmoved by it. Despite the pain sanctions inflicted, for many years he resisted the oil-for-food resolution, which was designed to alleviate the suffering of Iraq's people, to increase his chances of having all sanctions lifted and thus gain a political victory with his power base and increase his personal control over Iraq's economy. By some estimates, sanctions have already contributed to hundreds of thousands of deaths since the Gulf War (Mueller and Mueller, 1999, p. 43). If anything, Saddam views widespread suffering among Iraq's populace as a tool for gaining international (especially Arab) sympathy.

Military Defeat. The prospect of defeat on the battlefield shapes Saddam's tactics and the nature of his provocations. It is a sensitivity reflected in what Saddam does *not* do rather than observable Iraqi behavior. In theoretical terms, the prospect of military defeat deters Saddam from taking certain steps rather than coercing him to change his behavior. Saddam appears to understand that the military balance in the Gulf tilts against him. Saddam has not threatened his neighbors with his military forces since the 1994 buildup, which the United States countered with Operation Vigilant Warrior. The rapidity of the U.S. buildup, the strong ongoing U.S. regional presence, and the continuing weakness of Iraq's conventional forces probably led Saddam to conclude that another buildup would at best result in an Iraqi pullback and at worst the attrition of his forces.

The prospect of military defeat also heightens the chances of both elite dissatisfaction and popular unrest, making Saddam even less likely to issue challenges that could be met on the battlefield. Strikes on military forces could lead officers to become dissatisfied with Saddam, seeing his continued rule as a threat to their lives and prestige. His response to the 1998 Desert Fox strikes indicates that this fear has not abated despite his stronger position at home. In addition, dispersed military units are less able to suppress a coup or popular unrest, so Saddam is reluctant to provoke crises where he must disperse them. Saddam backed down (or, more accurately, did not press on) in 1996 after taking Irbil, for example, for fear of drawing U.S. strikes against his exposed forces.

Saddam has learned to avoid provocations that play to U.S. strengths, such as massing his armed forces to threaten his neighbors. He has not massed his forces since October 1994, and when he subsequently carried out offensive operations—as in August 1996—he used stealth to hide the buildup and quickly dispersed his troops once a threat became possible. Instead, he has focused on provocations regarding Iraq's NBC programs, which are far harder for the United States to counter with military strikes.

WHAT IRAQ IS *NOT* SENSITIVE TO

Several instruments intended to modulate Iraqi behavior appear to have little influence on Saddam. These include legal agreements, strikes on infrastructure, and tit-for-tat air campaigns.

Although it is widely understood that Saddam's Iraq cares little for legal niceties, the United States still focuses considerable attention on forcing Iraq to promise to respect various agreements. For example, Washington in 1994 pressed Iraq to recognize Kuwaiti sovereignty and the Kuwaiti border. It has also accepted Iraqi promises to cooperate with UNSCOM even though true cooperation never occurred.

Attention to legalities may win the United States points with its regional allies and the international community but will do little to influence Iraq's future behavior. Saddam's Iraq pursues a Machiavellian foreign policy in which a written agreement means nothing if it does not reflect the political realities of the moment. Thus, Saddam has repeatedly lied to UNSCOM inspectors, and Iraqi officials have indicated that their agreement over Kuwait's border is simply a scrap of paper. Such legal agreements and promises are not likely to affect Iraqi behavior in the future.

Infrastructure strikes also probably are of limited concern to Saddam. In general, strikes on infrastructure affect the Iraqi people, not the Iraqi regime: it is relatively easy to shield an elite few from the effect of power outages or other problems. Indeed, access to the regime's goodwill in the face of deprivations becomes even more vital and therefore a source of greater leverage, as economic infrastructure is degraded.

Finally, tit-for-tat strikes may actually encourage further Iraqi provocations. Strikes on air-defense systems and other strictly military targets pose little threat to regime stability but allow Saddam to demonstrate that he remains defiant toward the United States. Saddam probably has learned that the United States and its allies try to respect the principle of proportionality, and he may believe that such strikes erode the coalition on which the United States depends. Saddam may thus "win" politically despite modest operational damage.

IRAQI COUNTERMOVES TO OFFSET VULNERABILITIES

Saddam does not respond passively to U.S. attempts at coercion. Rather, he tries to tailor his response to exploit U.S. weaknesses whenever possible. The cases in Chapter Five reveal several typical Iraqi countermoves designed to neutralize coercive strategies. These include exploiting domestic suffering, complying incompletely with demands, trying to fracture coalitions, and repressing dissent.

Exploiting Domestic Suffering. Because the regime cares less about the welfare of ordinary Iraqis than do the coercing powers, Saddam can use them as hostages to alleviate coercive pressure. As mentioned earlier, the Baath regime has played up the suffering of the Iraqi people to gain sympathy in the Arab world and to undermine major power support for sanctions and other forms of coercion even as it resisted measures, such as the oil-for-food resolution, that would alleviate their suffering. The regime regularly exaggerated claims of the number of deaths from sanctions and from military strikes, even though it could easily have prevented any deaths through compliance had it so chosen. After coalition attacks, Saddam frequently mobilized his propaganda machine to try to play victim; Iraqi officials took foreign journalists to what they claimed were bombed civilian residences in an effort to generate international sympathy and foment international opposition to U.S. policy (Fineman, 1993a).[1]

Incomplete Compliance. Saddam regularly retreats from confrontations by making promises that he subsequently does not keep. Incomplete compliance puts the United States in an awkward position. As Washington discovered in November 1998 when it called off a bombing campaign at the last minute, it is difficult to coerce a foe who simply says yes, even if he then drags his feet in the execution phase or simply reneges. Incomplete compliance also makes it difficult to sustain coalition coercive strategies, especially as times goes by, because some coalition partners may be willing to accept submaximal concessions and imperfect compliance.

Incomplete compliance is a short-term gambit rather than a long-term strategy. Saddam's time horizons are short, and his timing is often clumsy and poor. The most obvious example of Saddam's mistakes were his actions regarding Iraq's NBC programs. Had Saddam declared his programs in 1991, inspections would have ended shortly and Saddam could quickly have rebuilt his programs. In 1997, Saddam could have adhered to the compromise engineered by UN Sec-

---

[1]For example, Saddam tried to use the accidental hotel bombing in January 1993 to whip up Arab anti-Washington sentiment (Gordon, 1993).

retary General Kofi Annan, under which he could have easily gotten a clean bill of health from a defanged UNSCOM regime. Instead, Saddam chose confrontation. Saddam will listen to advice from Russia, France, and other sympathizers and even modify his behavior accordingly as he did in 1997. However, if it does not result in quick improvements, he quickly reverts to his original strategy. In general, he is reactive in his approach. His 1996 incursion into Irbil capitalized on Kurdish infighting; he did not create the opportunity himself. This short-term perspective has often led Saddam to disrupt trends favorable to his regime.

Fracturing Coalitions. With mixed success, and only limited skill, Baghdad has tried to fracture the anti-Iraq coalition through a combination of inducements and threats. To woo Russia and France, Iraq has promised expedited debt payment and commercial concessions—once sanctions are lifted. In the Arab world, Saddam has tried to appeal directly to the Arab people, using the widespread anti-U.S. sentiment to rally support and press their governments. At times, he has also excoriated regional governments, hoping to frighten them into abandoning their support for the United States. To satisfy these potential allies, Saddam has used partial compliance to demonstrate his goodwill.

Saddam's coalition-splitting efforts would have been more successful at undermining U.S.-led strategies if he were as adept at manipulating foreign relations as he is at manipulating internal political ones. Saddam regularly lambastes or criticizes U.S. allies and their leadership, hoping to intimidate them into cooperation. For example, the Iraqi Foreign Minister in May 1994 called Saudi King Fahd a feeble-minded alcoholic and claimed that the House of Saud is of Jewish descent (Baram, 1998, p. 141). After Desert Fox, the Iraqi regime lashed out at Turkey, Saudi Arabia, and Egypt, calling their regimes illegitimate. Not surprisingly, these blasts produce a hostile response. Saudi press, which generally avoids criticism of any sort, blamed Saddam personally for Iraq's many problems, in essence condoning the U.S. position of confrontation (Baram, 1998, p. 142). Turkey and Egypt, which had been increasingly sympathetic to Iraq's position, quickly moved back toward the U.S. camp.

Saddam's attempts to appeal to the "Arab Street" on pan-Arab, anti-U.S. grounds also have met with little success. Baghdad has portrayed its opponents as tools of Israel and cast its propaganda in Arab and Muslim terms. Although most Arab states are sensitive to Arab and Islamic issues, public opinion of this kind has only limited effect on Arab state policymaking. Islamic radicals who might otherwise support Saddam also are skeptical of his calls for *jihad* because of his ruthless suppression of religion within Iraq.

Repressing Dissent. To offset threats from his power base or from the Iraqi people, Saddam ruthlessly clamps down on any unrest. He does not hesitate to kill, torture, imprison, or exile opponents on a wide scale at the mere suspicion of disloyalty. He also systematically prevents any individual from forming an independent power base that could challenge his rule.

Repression of this kind, in addition to offsetting some forms of domestic pressure in the short term, has potentially adverse consequences for Saddam and for those trying to coerce him. As a result of his brutal efforts to retain control, Saddam lacks access to informed and honest advisors. Instead he surrounds himself with sycophants who support his policies unquestioningly. This may explain his poor timing and in particular his tendency to miscalculate about events outside Iraq. In October 1994, just when the UN Security Council was meeting to consider the removal of sanctions, Iraq began a multidivision buildup on the Iraq-Kuwait border, killing any chance for relief that Saddam might have had. Similarly, in 1998 he continued to openly defy UNSCOM even after he had already gained the sympathy of Russia, China, and France, forcing them to reluctantly support the use of force.

The above discussion of Iraq's vulnerabilities illuminates challenges inherent to coercing Iraq. On the one hand, striking at Iraq's power base is the most effective and proven means of moving the regime. On the other hand, fine-tuning the political impact of U.S. attacks is difficult, especially given Saddam's predictable and unpredictable countermoves. Even slightly misdirected U.S. pressure has at times backfired, leading to greater Iraqi intransigence or instances of the very behavior the United States sought to prevent.

Chapter Seven

IMPLICATIONS FOR COERCION

The Iraqi experience is rich with general lessons for coercing major regional powers in critical regions. Although successful coercion is as much art as science, the Iraqi experience instructs policymakers to pay particular attention to several key issues in designing coercive strategies. These include an understanding of the adversary's centers of gravity, factors the United States *cannot* realistically change, the dynamic nature of coercion contests, the need to integrate coercive threats into long-term policy, and self-imposed limits on the U.S. use of force. This chapter addresses the broader implications of the Iraq experience to aid the design of future coercive strategies.

RECOGNIZING ADVERSARY CENTERS OF GRAVITY

When planning a coercive strategy, policymakers should strive to identify the target's "center of gravity"—that which, if destroyed, would cause the enemy's resistance to collapse. For Iraq, this appears to be Saddam's relationship with his power base. When coercive threats placed pressure on Iraq's center, they proved far more likely to move the regime.

A center of gravity will vary by regime. In a democracy, the number of people with input into decisionmaking is vast. Successful coercion might therefore focus on the opinion of the majority or the country's economic health. Authoritarian regimes, however, have different pressure points. Sanctions, infrastructure strikes, and other pressures that affect an entire country often fail or even backfire because they affect elites and nonelites differently. Iraq suffers when a bridge is blown up, but the regime is often unaffected. The less democratic the country, the more important such distinctions. When the ruling elite can ignore the wishes of the people, coercive threats should focus accordingly.

Threatening a center of gravity can be a two-edged sword. A danger is that the adversary may view escalation, or at least continued defiance, as the best way to protect its center of gravity. Planning should therefore focus on the adversary's center of gravity not only to inform the way the United States threatens the adversary but to anticipate its likely responses.

A better understanding of Iraq's or another adversary's center of gravity would lead to more effective targeting and strategy in general. Striking certain targets, such as air-defense sites, does little for coercion, though they may have substantial benefits for other objectives or to make future coercive uses of forces easier or more credible. Strikes on regime security forces, elite military units, or other regime pillars, however, can lead to concessions out of proportion to the damage inflicted. Economic measures also should focus on the country's center of gravity, recognizing that different types of sanctions and financial restrictions affect different parts of a populace (Kirshner, 1997).

COERCION AS A DYNAMIC PROCESS

The need to anticipate adversary responses to coercion raises a second major point to guide strategy-making: coercion is a dynamic encounter. It should be thought of not as one state manipulating another with threats but as two or more states each simultaneously trying to alter the decisionmaking of others. The coercive contest may be brief, or it may unfold gradually.

Planning must acknowledge that just as the United States is (or should be) performing a "center of gravity" analysis on the adversary, the adversary is likely doing the same on the United States or the coalition aligned against it. Many adversaries probably view public support as the U.S. center of gravity. Hence, adversaries are likely to target that support actively, adopting strategies likely to erode it. When coalition support is critical to the U.S. strategy, coalition unity may be viewed as a center of gravity vulnerable to attack. By threatening this unity—whether through limited concessions, aggressive actions aimed at vulnerable members, or propaganda offensives exploiting collateral damage resulting from U.S. attacks—an adversary may seek to counter-coerce the United States. Just as when the United States threatens an adversary's center of gravity, the goal is not necessarily to destroy it. An adversary need not actually break American public support or coalition unity, because the threat of such occurrences could be enough to end U.S. efforts or sufficiently offset U.S. pressure. U.S. decisionmakers generally anticipate threats to U.S. centers of gravity and limit the scope and scale of U.S. attacks to evade them.

Another aspect to the dynamism of coercion is the change in stakes that may occur during the course of crises. The Iraq experience vividly demonstrates not only that U.S. goals change—they can, and will in most long-term coercive contests—but also that coercive threats themselves can create new stakes. In creating no-fly zones, the U.S. stakes were largely derived from humanitarian concerns. But once the United States committed to enforcing them, it put its credibility on the line. Suddenly, responding to Iraqi violations was a matter of far deeper concern, because failure to do so might signal weakness to Saddam. Such an escalation of stakes was perhaps unavoidable. U.S. policymakers tried through their rhetoric to distance themselves from commitments to the Kurds, for example, with little success. Although the escalation of stakes was not intentional, it could have been anticipated through better analysis and, in turn, prepared-for more properly.

Because of shifting objectives, defining and assessing victory is difficult. Containment has largely worked since 1991. Saddam's constant low-level challenges and provocations, however, make it hard to portray U.S. policy as successful. Over time some policies become victims of their own success—they are criticized as failures despite meeting their most basic objectives.

U.S. credibility is constantly at stake, whether Washington acts or not, and the actions taken in one crisis have consequences for subsequent standoffs. The limited Desert Strike response to Saddam's incursion into Irbil probably emboldened the Iraqi leader, convincing him that any U.S. response to future provocations would be limited. Similarly, a failure to react to repeated interference with UNSCOM in 1996 and 1997 may have contributed to Saddam's decision to reject all cooperation in 1998. Appreciating the shifting nature of stakes and credibility is critical when seeking to contain a major regional power, which is likely to probe and provoke the United States over many issues and over the course of many years.

UNDERSTANDING WHAT CANNOT BE AFFECTED

The United States can affect only the level of pain it inflicts, not an adversary's willingness to accept it. Ho Chi Minh's often-quoted statement that the North Vietnamese could endure ten times as many casualties as the United States and nevertheless triumph strikes at the essence of many failed coercive strategies: a misunderstanding of the adversary's willingness to accept punishment. Adversary regimes with little popular input or those that capitalize on anti-U.S. nationalism can often endure tremendous suffering. The willingness to take punishment may fluctuate over time. Saddam's ability and willingness to accept punishment grew as his position at home became stronger.

Neither are some adversary regimes willing to give up power. If Saddam and his henchmen stepped down, they would likely lose their lives as well as their privileges. Although a national strategy that seeks regime change may be sensible, it is difficult to coerce such a change when the costs of compliance seem intolerably greater than any strikes the United States could mete out.

Coercing populations to revolt or elites to carry out a coup is extremely difficult to engineer. The police and enforcement powers of Saddam's Iraq or other regimes are extensive; authoritarian regimes will kill and torture families and communities, not just the individuals in question. Suffering continued U.S. military strikes is almost always a far safer option for would-be oppositionists. Moreover, military strikes often provoke a nationalist backlash, increasing support at least in the short term for a regime among the populace and among elites.

INTEGRATING COERCIVE THREATS INTO LONG-TERM POLICY

The recurring U.S. difficulties in confronting Iraq illustrate a broader challenge for U.S. policy: planning for the long-term. Initial assessments about the fragility of Saddam's regime were based on sound premises and analysis. The Iraqi dictator nevertheless survived. Policymakers and analysts did not prepare for what may have been a low probability event, creating problems in sustaining the anti-Iraq alliance over time.

Planning for the long term and integrating coercive threats into broader planning are easier said than done. Several steps, however, are critical to better planning and integration in future confrontations:

- Preparing "what ifs" to challenge conventional policy. Intelligence should focus on low-probability but high-impact events. The intention is to make policy as robust as possible, preparing for contingencies today even if they do not materialize. For Iraq, such events today might include Saddam's assassination, Iraq's fragmentation after a civil war, the emergence of a Shi'a-led Iraq, or another Iraqi foray into the north.

- Conducting "red team" analysis to understand an adversary's perspective. This should be conducted on a political as well as operational level, trying to understand an adversary's motivations and how it might respond to various U.S. coercive threats.

- Anticipating policy shifts. Planning should also consider the likelihood that U.S. objectives will change. U.S. objectives often shift, leading to a potential disconnect between U.S. policy ends and means. The success of certain policies can lead decisionmakers to focus on more ambitious objectives. Once it became clear that a major Iraqi ground incursion was unlikely, attention focused on other, more plausible threats, such as Iraq's NBC arsenal and Saddam himself. A change in objectives, however, is not always accompanied by a coherent overall policy. U.S. attempts to replace the regime in Baghdad, for example, have little support among U.S. allies, thus undermining containment and the prospect of renewed NBC inspections. The priorities of allies, and U.S. domestic support, do not always shift in accord with changing administration objectives.

RECOGNIZING OUR OWN LIMITS

Attempts to coerce Iraq reveal the degree to which self-imposed constraints, especially those generated by political and diplomatic concerns, limit the quantity and type of force the United States can threaten or use.

Domestic support for operations against Iraq has generally been high. Neither the Bush nor the Clinton administration faced criticism for expanding the U.S. regional presence or for conducting limited strikes against Iraq. But a fear that this support might dissipate in the face of casualties probably drove policymakers to use cruise missiles when other instruments might not only have delivered greater material effect but also demonstrated a more credible U.S. willingness to incur costs. Similar reasoning also led decisionmakers to avoid larger deployments or measures that would lead to a long-term U.S. presence in a potentially hostile region.

Because of strong domestic support, U.S. credibility is likely to be high when confronting major regional powers over vital interests, but its overall policy flexibility may be limited. Calls for an aggressive U.S. policy are likely, making the administration's threats to use force highly believable. But backing down, even over issues not vital to U.S. interests or combining threats with concessions or positive inducements may be politically impossible.

A far greater limit to the U.S. use of force against Iraq—one that tended to severely weaken resolve and lessen credibility—was the constraints allies placed on coercive threats. When the major powers and regional allies spoke with one voice, as they did in the aftermath of the Gulf War, Saddam listened. As coalition fractiousness increased, however, Saddam increasingly believed he could end Iraq's isolation and sanctions by courting a few key members, particularly France and Russia. To maintain coalition unity and placate wary members, the United States often limited its use of force. Perhaps the most extensive limits were visible after Saddam's northern incursion in September 1996, when a lack of regional basing and little major power support made it difficult for the United States to launch a sustained operation against Iraq without sacrificing coalition unity.[1] Of course, broader strategic considerations may require bringing and keeping certain members in a coalition. However, if doing so severely undermines the potency and credibility of forceful options, overall policy must be reassessed.

The need to retain domestic and allied support can generate negative objectives that shape U.S. policy. As in Iraq, the United States may seek to avoid destabilizing an ally—a concern that may limit the scope and nature of any military strike.

The political and diplomatic constraints just enumerated offer planners difficult balancing calculations. On the one hand, public and coalition support is generally necessary to sustain coercion strategies, especially over time. At some point, efforts to maintain that support may become so burdensome and the adverse consequences for military effectiveness so great that the strategy as a whole is neutralized. In such circumstances, the United States should consider reducing its reliance on multinational coalitions and focus instead on retaining the support of a core group of states. In Iraq, such an effort might enable the United States to conduct more sustained strikes against the regime when necessary and, given the demise of effective inspections, would cost Washington little with regard to programs that require international support.

By adopting the framework developed in this study, policymakers can design more sustainable, more robust, and ultimately more effective coercive strategies. Equally important, it will help policymakers avoid situations where coercive threats will fail in the short term and undermine the credibility of future U.S. threats.

---

[1]Whereas coalition disagreements over how to respond to Iraqi transgressions generally put *downward* pressure on the level of coercive force practically available to decisionmakers, the reverse may have been true in some later cases. During the 1997–1998 inspections standoff, for example, most Arab nations publicly condemned the U.S. stance of military threats. However, their governments intimated that, while they did not support limited strikes likely only to provoke Iraqi hostility, they would welcome robust strikes that truly incapacitated Saddam's regime.

BIBLIOGRAPHY

Achen, Christopher H., and Duncan Snidal, "Rational Deterrence Theory and Comparative Case Studies," *World Politics,* Vol. 41, No. 2, January 1989, pp. 143–169.

Albright, Joseph, "U.S., Allies to Enforce No-Fly Zone in S. Iraq," *Atlanta Journal-Constitution,* August 26, 1992, p. A1.

Al-Quds al'Arabi, "Egyptian-Iraqi Agreement on 'Qualitative and Quiet Shift in Relations,'" September 25, 1996.

Al-Sharq al-Awsat, "Iranian Role in Kurdistan Events Viewed," September 4, 1996a.

_____, "Interview with Egyptian Foreign Minister 'Amr Musa," September 24, 1996b.

Al-Watan al-Arabi, "Hussein Kamil on Army Strength, Saddam Fedayeen," November 24, 1995, in FBIS-NES-95-227, November, 27, 1995, p. 33.

Associated Press, "Commander Opposes White House Strategy to Topple Saddam," January 28, 1999, accessed from http:/www.joplinglobe.com/iraq/iraq9.html.

Baker, James, "Hearings on the Current Situation in Iraq," testimony before the Senate Armed Services Committee, September 12, 1996.

Baldwin, David, "The Power of Positive Sanctions," *World Politics,* Vol. 24, No. 1, October 1971, pp. 19–38.

Baram, Amatzia, *Building Toward Crises: Saddam Hussein's Strategy for Survival*, Washington, D.C.: Washington Institute for Near East Policy, 1998.

Bar-Joseph, Uri, "Variations on a Theme: The Conceptualization of Deterrence in Israeli Strategic Thinking," *Security Studies*, Vol. 7, No. 3, Spring 1998, pp. 145–181.

Bar-Siman-Tov, Yaacov, "The War of Attrition, 1969–1970," in Alexander L. George, ed., *Avoiding War: Problems of Crisis Management*, Boulder, Colo.: Westview Press, 1991, pp. 320–341.

Beijing Central People's Radio Network, "Commentary Condemns U.S. Attack on Iraq," September 17, 1996, broadcast.

Bengio, Ofra, *Saddam's Word: Political Discourse in Iraq*, New York: Oxford University Press, 1998.

Buchan, David, "France Criticizes US Cruise Missile Attack on Baghdad," *Financial Times*, January 21, 1993, p. 1.

Bueno de Mesquita, Bruce, *The War Trap*, New Haven, Conn.: Yale University Press, 1981.

Byman, Daniel, "Let Iraq Collapse," *The National Interest*, No. 45, Fall 1996, pp. 48–60.

_____, "Proceed with Caution: U.S. Support for the Iraqi Opposition," *The Washington Quarterly*, June 1999a, pp. 23–37.

_____, interview with U.S. government official, 1999b.

Byman, Daniel, and Jerrold Green, *Political Violence in the States of the Northern Persian Gulf*, Santa Monica, Calif.: RAND, MR-1021-OSD, 1999.

Byman, Daniel, Kenneth Pollack, and Gideon Rose, "The Rollback Fantasy," *Foreign Affairs*, Vol. 78, No. 1, January/February 1999, pp. 24–41.

Byman, Daniel, Kenneth Pollack, and Matthew Waxman, "Coercing Saddam Hussein: Lessons from the Past," *Survival*, Vol. 40, No. 3, Autumn 1998, pp. 127–152.

Byman, Daniel, and Matthew Waxman, "Defeating U.S. Coercion," *Survival,* Vol. 41, No. 2, Summer 1999, pp. 107–120.

Byman, Daniel, Matthew Waxman, and Eric Larson, *Air Power as a Coercive Instrument,* Santa Monica, Calif.: RAND, MR-1061-AF, 1999.

Clinton, William J., "Clinton's Statement: 'We Are Delivering a Powerful Message to Saddam,'" *New York Times,* December 17, 1998, p. A16.

Cockburn, Andrew, and Patrick Cockburn, *Out of the Ashes: The Resurrection of Saddam Hussein,* New York: HarperCollins, 1999.

"Congressional Letter to the President of the United States," June 22, 1998.

Connelly, Marjorie, "Wide U.S. Support for Air Strikes," *New York Times,* December 18, 1998, p. A26.

Cordesman, Anthony, "Hearings on the Current Situation in Iraq," testimony before the Senate Armed Services Committee, September 12, 1996.

Cowell, Alan, "Baghdad Formally Agrees to 'Unjust' U.N. Conditions for Permanent Cease-Fire," *New York Times,* April 7, 1991, p. A1.

Crossette, Barbara, "Iraq's Attempt to Have Sanctions Lifted Quickly May Have Backfired," *New York Times,* October 11, 1994, p. A13.

_____, "As Tension Grows, Few Voices at U.N. Speak Up for Iraq," *New York Times,* November 13, 1998a, p. A6.

_____, "U.S. Welcomes Arab Statement on Iraq," *New York Times,* November 13, 1998b, p. A14.

Department of Defense, news briefing, December 16, 1998.

Deutch, John, testimony before the Senate Select Intelligence Committee, September 19, 1996.

Djerejian, Edward, "Developments in the Middle East," testimony before the Subcommittee on Europe and the Middle East of the

Foreign Affairs Committee, U.S. House of Representatives, November 20, 1991.

Drozdiak, William, "France Implies Domestic Politics in U.S. Sparked Response to Iraq," *Washington Post*, October 13, 1994, p. A29.

Eisenstadt, Michael, "U.S. Policy Toward Iraq: Balance, Dismember, or Contain?" testimony before the National Security Subcommittee, U.S. House of Representatives, September 26, 1996.

Eisenstadt, Michael, and Kenneth Pollack, "The Crisis with Iraq: Reviving the Military Options," *PolicyWatch*, Washington Institute for Near East Policy, No. 295, January 22, 1998.

El Reedy, Abdel Raouf, "Striking the Right Balance," *Guardian Weekly*, January 31, 1993, p. 6.

Ergin, Sedat, "Khoja Erkaban Cautions United States: Do Not Strike," *Istanbul Hürriyet*, September 20, 1996.

"Evolution of U.S. Policy on Iraq, the Iraqi Opposition, and Northern Iraq," *PolicyWatch*, Washington Institute for Near East Policy, No. 219, September 19, 1996.

Fineman, Mark, "Iraq's Propaganda Machine Cranks Up," *Los Angeles Times*, January 16, 1993a, p. A6.

_____, "Hussein's Moves Seen as Steps in Calculated Plan," *Los Angeles Times*, January 17, 1993b, p. A1.

Freedman, Lawrence, and Efraim Karsh, *The Gulf Conflict 1990–1991*, Princeton, N.J.: Princeton University Press, 1993.

Gause, F. Gregory, III, "Saddam's Unwatched Arsenal," *Foreign Affairs*, Vol. 78, No. 3, May/June 1999, pp. 54–65.

Gellman, Barton, "U.S. Committed to Change in Baghdad, Berger Says," *Washington Post*, December 9, 1998.

George, Alexander, and William E. Simons, eds., *The Limits of Coercive Diplomacy*, Boulder, Colo.: Westview Press, 1994.

Gonzalez, M., and I. Cembrero, "More on Refusal to Allow U.S. to Use Base," *El Pais*, September 14, 1996.

Gordon, Michael R., "U.S. Leads Further Attacks on Iraqi Antiaircraft Sites; Admits Its Missile Hit Hotel," *New York Times*, January 19, 1993, p. A1.

Grier, Peter, "Where Players Stand After Iraq Crisis," *Christian Science Monitor*, November 21, 1997, p. 1.

Gunter, Michael M., "The KDP-PUK Conflict in Northern Iraq," *Middle East Journal*, Vol. 50, No. 2, 1996, pp. 225–241.

Haass, Richard N., "U.S. Policy Toward Iraq: Balance, Dismember, or Contain?" testimony before the National Security Subcommittee, U.S. House of Representatives, September 26, 1996.

Healy, Melissa, "Clinton Urged to Weigh Heavier Attacks on Iraq," *Los Angeles Times*, January 19, 1993, p. A1.

Herr, W. Eric, "Operation Vigilant Warrior: Conventional Deterrence Theory, Doctrine, and Practice," School of Advanced Airpower Studies thesis, Maxwell AFB, Ala.: June 1996.

Hopf, Ted, *Peripheral Visions: Deterrence Theory and American Foreign Policy in the Third World, 1965–1990,* Ann Arbor, Mich.: University of Michigan Press, 1994.

Horner, Gen. Charles A., USAF (Ret.), "What We Should Have Learned in Desert Storm, But Didn't," *Air Force Magazine,* Vol. 79, No. 12, 1996, accessed from http://www.afa.org/magazine/21_century/desert_storm

Huth, Paul K., "Reputations and Deterrence," *Security Studies*, Vol. 7, No. 1, Fall 1997, pp. 72–99.

Interfax, "Moscow 'Working with Baghdad,' Urging Restraint," September 14, 1996.

Iraqi News Agency, "Defense Minister Views U.S. Attack, 'Split' in Alliance," September 23, 1996.

Jehl, Douglas, "U.S. Fighters in Saudi Arabia Grounded," *New York Times*, December 19, 1998, p. A9.

Kahneman, Daniel, and Amos Tversky, "Prospect Theory: An Analysis of Decision Under Risk," *Econometrica*, Vol. 47, No. 2, 1979, pp. 263–291.

Kelly, John, "United States Policy Toward the Middle East and the Persian Gulf," testimony before the House Committee on Foreign Affairs, June 26, 1991.

Khalilzad, Zalmay, "The United States and the Persian Gulf: Preventing Regional Hegemony," *Survival*, Vol. 37, No. 2, Summer 1995, pp. 95–120.

Kirshner, Jonathan, "The Microfoundations of Economic Sanctions," *Security Studies*, Vol. 6, No. 3, Spring 1997, pp. 32–64.

Kremp, Herbert, "Europe Is Sinking under the Horizon of U.S. Politics," *Welt am Sonntag,* September 29, 1996.

Lancaster, John, "U.S. Moves to Toughen Iraq Stance," *Washington Post*, August 29, 1992, p. A1.

Lewis, Paul, "U.S.-Led Raids on Iraq Strain Unity of Gulf War Coalition," *New York Times*, January 20, 1993, p. A1.

Lieberman, Elli, "What Makes Deterrence Work: Lessons from the Egyptian-Israeli Enduring Rivalry," *Security Studies*, Vol. 4, No. 4, Summer 1995, pp. 833–892.

Matlak, Regis W., "Inside Saddam's Grip," *National Security Studies Quarterly,* Spring 1999, accessed from http://www.georgetown.edu/sfs/programs/nssp/nssq/Matlak.pdf

McDowall, David, *A Modern History of the Kurds*, London: I. B. Taurus, 1996.

Melloan, George, "A Few Guesses About What's on Saddam's Mind," *Wall Street Journal,* October 10, 1994, p. A13.

Meyers, Steven Lee, "U.S. Forces Set to Strike Iraq in Hours If Called On," *New York Times*, November 18, 1998, p. A8.

Miller, Charles, "Britain, France, U.S. Send 'Clear Warning' to Saddam," Press Association, September 16, 1996.

Morgan, Patrick M., *Deterrence: A Conceptual Analysis*, Beverly Hills, Calif: Sage Library of Social Science, 1977.

_____, "Saving Face for the Sake of Deterrence," in Robert Jervis, Richard Ned Lebow, and Janice Gross Stein, eds., *Psychology & Deterrence*, Baltimore, Md.: Johns Hopkins University Press, 1985, pp. 125–152.

Mueller, John, and Karl Mueller, "The Real Weapons of Mass Destruction." *Foreign Affairs*, Vol. 78, No. 3, May/June 1999.

Murphy, Caryle, "Saudi Air Force Aiding U.S. in Enforcement Operation Over Iraq," *Washington Post*, August 30, 1992, p. A32.

Pape, Robert A., *Bombing to Win*, Ithaca, N.Y.: Cornell University Press, 1996.

Perle, Richard, "U.S. Policy Toward Iraq: Balance, Dismember, or Contain?" testimony before the National Security Subcommittee, U.S. House of Representatives, September 26, 1996.

Riding, Alan, "Europeans Urging Enclave for Kurds in Northern Iraq," *New York Times*, April 9, 1991, p. A1.

Riedel, Bruce, "U.S. Policy Toward Iraq: Balance, Dismember, or Contain?" testimony before the National Security Subcommittee, U.S. House of Representatives, September 26, 1996.

Ritter, Scott, 1999. *Endgame: Solving the Iraq Problem Once and for All*, New York: Simon & Schuster, 1999.

Robinson, Eugene, "Criticism from Gulf War Allies Strains U.S.-Led Coalition," *Washington Post*, January 20, 1993, p. A25.

Sayari, Sabri, statement before the Subcommittees on Arms Control, International Security, and Science and on Europe and the Middle East of the Committee on Foreign Affairs, U.S. House of Representatives, April 11, 1991, as it appears in "Post-War Policy Issues in the Persian Gulf," Washington, D.C.: U.S. Government Printing Office, 1991.

Scheffer, David J., statement before the Subcommittee on Near Eastern and South Asian Affairs, Committee on Foreign Relations, U.S.

Senate, May 10, 1991, as it appears in "The Middle East," Washington, D.C.: U.S. Government Printing Office, 1991.

Schelling, Thomas, *Arms and Influence,* New Haven, Conn.: Yale University Press, 1966.

Schmitt, Eric, "Gulf Syndrome: Americans Decide War May Not Be Quite So Scary," *New York Times,* November 30, 1997, Sec. 4, p. 1.

Sciolino, Elaine, "Iraqi Report Says Chemical Arsenal Survived the War," *New York Times,* April 20, 1991, p. A1.

_____, "Kuwait Crisis: Hussein Gambles to Keep Power," *New York Times,* October 11, 1994, p. A13.

Shalikashvili, Gen. John M., USA (Ret.), interview, 1999.

Shimshoni, Jonathan, *Israel and Conventional Deterrence: Border Warfare from 1953–1970,* Ithaca, N.Y.: Cornell University Press, 1988.

Stein, Janice Gross, "Deterrence and Compellence in the Gulf, 1990–1991," *International Security,* Vol. 17, No. 2, Fall 1992.

_____, "The Arab-Israeli War of 1967: Inadvertent War Through Miscalculated Escalation," in Alexander L. George, ed., *Avoiding War: Problems of Crisis Management,* Boulder, Colo.: Westview Press, 1991, pp. 126–159.

Steinberg, Gerald, "U.S. Responses to the Proliferation of Weapons of Mass Destruction in the Middle East," *Middle East Review of International Affairs,* Vol. 2, No. 3, September 1998, accessed from http://www.biu.ac.il/SOC/besa/meria/journal/1998/issue3/jv2n3 a4.html

Telhami, Shibley, "U.S. Iraqi Policy Alienating Arab Allies," *Los Angeles Times,* November 30, 1997, p. M2.

_____, "Kuwait Crisis: Hussein Gambles to Keep Power," *New York Times,* October 11, 1994, p. A13.

Urquhart, Brian, "How Not to Fight a Dictator," *New York Review of Books,* May 6, 1999, pp. 25–29.

Watts, David, "West's 'Double Standards' Rouse Arab Suspicions; Plan for a Kurdish Safe Haven," *The Times* (London), April 10, 1991.

Wright, Robin, "U.S. Officials Concede That Discord Within 29-Nation Alliance Served to Limit Actions Against Iraq," *Los Angeles Times,* January 19, 1993.

Wurmser, David, *Tyranny's Ally*, Washington, D.C.: The AEI Press, 1999.